Your History, Your Future

Your History, Your Future

An Insider's Guide to Background Investigations

ANTHONY OATIS

ROWMAN & LITTLEFIELD
Lanham • Boulder • New York • London

Published by Rowman & Littlefield
An imprint of The Rowman & Littlefield Publishing Group, Inc.
4501 Forbes Boulevard, Suite 200, Lanham, Maryland 20706
www.rowman.com

6 Tinworth Street, London, SE11 5AL, United Kingdom

British Library Cataloguing in Publication Information Available

Library of Congress Cataloging-in-Publication Data

Names: Oatis, Anthony, 1959– author.
Title: Your history, your future : an insider's guide to background investigations / Anthony Oatis.
Description: Lanham : Rowman & Littlefield, 2021. | Includes bibliographical references and index. | Summary: "Most young adults know little about background checks, despite their use by schools and employers. This book guides readers through the process. It explains the consequences of infractions, what to expect during the background check, how to prepare for interviews, and what to do if you already have an infraction on your record"— Provided by publisher.
Identifiers: LCCN 2021008375 (print) | LCCN 2021008376 (ebook) | ISBN 9781538132838 (hardback) | ISBN 9781538132845 (ebook)
Subjects: LCSH: Employee screening.
Classification: LCC HF5549.5.E429 O28 2021 (print) | LCC HF5549.5.E429 (ebook) | DDC 650.14—dc23
LC record available at https://lccn.loc.gov/2021008375
LC ebook record available at https://lccn.loc.gov/2021008376

Contents

1

Why You Need This Book

"Actions have consequences!"

Who hasn't heard this phrase, often exclaimed by a parent to a son or daughter for a minor (pun intended) infraction? Parents utter this warning to teach their children to *think* before they act—to consider what might result from careless misbehavior. Getting grounded by your father for staying out late is one thing, and maybe you learned your lesson. But it's an altogether different proposition when your actions come back to haunt you years after your transgression is a faded memory.

If you think that what you do today won't matter a year from now, two years from now, or several years down the line, *think again*.

You may have moved on, but it's forever a part of your history. Your history is much like your shadow: you may not be aware of it, but it's with you all of the time, and you can see it best when the light is shining on you.

That prank you pulled with your friends on a fellow classmate—the one the police blew all out of proportion? It's still out there.

That shoplifting charge that was dropped after you logged in twenty-four hours of community service? It's still out there.

That joking rant about the president you posted on Facebook, the one that caught the attention of the FBI? It's still out there.

Recent college graduates seeking employment know enough to prepare a resume to submit to prospective employers. They compile one that will highlight their education, GPA, part-time jobs, internships, volunteer activities, and accomplishments. Of course, employers want to know what *you* think makes you a good candidate. And they will direct their human resources department to check the references you offered to find out what others think of you as well. You might look good on paper, so they'll call you in for an interview to find out more about you. But most companies also want to know what you *didn't* say on your resume and what you neglected to mention in your interview. They will conduct what they call "due diligence."

This is a book about that due diligence.

This is a book about consequences—*your* consequences.

This is a book about a stranger, an investigator you don't know (and likely will never meet) whose job it is to find out not only if you are qualified to *work* for a *Fortune* 500 company—even as the lowest-level grunt in the mailroom—but if you *belong* in the company. That investigator will be looking at everything you do and everything you *did*. Finding out all about you is his job. And he takes that job very seriously. For him, looking into your history is just one part of a process—a background investigation process.

You, like most high school and college students, probably don't know much about a background investigation process. Perhaps some students have a vague idea that a process takes place, but that's likely where their knowledge starts and ends. Most people applying for a job, admission to a school or other program, a loan at a bank or a credit card, even an unpaid internship, have little or no understanding of how the process works. Worse: they may realize too late that their past is now the main topic of discussion, a topic that will determine their future opportunities in life.

But ignorance is no defense.

This is a book about the process.

This is a book about the what, the where, and the when. It's about the how and the why. It most definitely starts with the who, and that who is *you*.

I wrote this book to help you.

KNOWLEDGE POINT

A background investigation or background check is the process of creating a report containing all the information of a person's history relating to employment, education, criminal activity, and finances. The process doesn't rely only on what the applicant reveals but requires that an investigator dig into the applicant's history independently. There are different terms for different kinds of background investigations. A credit check is an investigation of only financial history, while a security clearance for the government investigates everything in a person's past.

Young people coming and going through the activities of life. *Orbon Alija/E+ via Getty Images*

WHAT TO EXPECT

In this book, I'm going to walk you through the background investigation process. I'm going to help you think about the consequences of your actions as they relate to that process. There are short-term consequences and long-term consequences. It's often the long-term consequences that have the biggest effect but are the most difficult to see. I'm going to help you see a bigger picture than you might otherwise have seen.

Part of making good decisions comes from knowing your options. Part comes from understanding consequences. Since, as a young person, you may lack life experience, I'm hoping I can provide in this book some things to think about when facing difficult decisions. It's all right not to know something. When you discover you don't know, stop to consider how you can find out.

Remember, if you are not willing to admit mistakes, then you are prone to repeat bad choices. Also, if you do not take ownership of bad choices, you tend to exhibit self-deception by assigning these bad choices to reasons outside of your control. In other words, you blame others for your mistakes.

KNOWLEDGE POINT

Asking for help or advice is not a sign of weakness. Think about how a doctor, lawyer, judge, or teacher will gather information, seek advice, and then consider their options before making a decision. *You* are in charge of your past, present, and future life choices; you also need to collect information when trying to make a decision. Gather the best information, seek out the best advice, then choose the best course of action for you.

When I was a high school student, nobody talked to me about how life choices could have a negative impact on my admissions to college or entry into the military. Nobody provided a "Do Not Do" list. The focus in high school was graduating with the grades to be admitted into college. Of course, when I was a student, nobody was posting their entire life on the Internet. There was no Internet. Information that today is available to anyone with a computer was, back then, much more difficult to find. I had the perception that it didn't matter what I did as a kid. I could "get away with stuff." It wasn't really true then. It isn't true now. Choices matter.

Throughout this book, I'm going to tell you a lot of stories about young people I've encountered, the bad choices they made, and the consequences of those choices. The point of these stories is to get you thinking about choices you make in your life and, I hope, to help you avoid making the wrong choices. What if you've already made some bad choices? What if you read some of these stories and think to yourself, "Oh boy, I did that. I've already done that. What happens now?" Well, nobody is perfect. Everybody makes mistakes. All through your life, you will make mistakes, bad decisions, and poor choices (along with the good!). What matters is how you choose to deal with them. You can recover from many bad choices. Later in the book, I will tell you how you can help yourself.

Let me tell you some facts about what you will be facing when you go out to apply for college, for your first job (or any job), or to join the military. The US government created the background investigation process to "verify that the applicant does not have a history of activity that would make them unsuitable for the position for which they are being considered."[1] The process of checking on employment applicants (and now college applicants and, really, applicants for almost anything in the modern world) has become commonplace. This was not always so. It used to be that background checks were only performed for sensitive jobs in law enforcement and the government. It wasn't until the assassination attempt on President Ronald Reagan in 1981 that a coordinated background investigation process became common. Of course, the terrorist attacks on September 11, 2001, raised the bar on security concerns a lot! What started as a simple "check" of a person's recent activities has become a comprehensive review of a person's history back to their eighteenth birthday.

Background investigations serve several purposes. They provide the requester (that could be a potential employer, school, or even a credit card company) with the information necessary to be sure the candidate (you) is not a criminal. They also provide the "peace of mind" that the applicant is being truthful and has demonstrated good judgment throughout their life. Today's corporate, college, and government institutions believe that they are entitled to know all details of prospective candidates' lives, beyond the limits of past criminal convictions. What you do; who you text, call, or e-mail; what you post online, all provide a picture of who you are. All can be used for or against you later in your life.

Today's background investigations can furnish almost everything anyone would want to know about you. Background investigations today access criminal databases, court records, sex-offender registries, employment history (part and full time), critical screening for driver's licenses, educational history (records from elementary school through high school), and even community organizations and churches. With today's technology and sharing of information from both the private and government sectors, the result is an unlimited access to your past history. The background investigation process is here to stay, and as our technology and communications systems become more integrated and advanced, your social media activities and past history will be more available to anyone who knows where to look.

Passing a background check is critical to getting hired for a job. An employer doesn't want to hire someone they think will use bad judgment, be dishonest, or, worse, act criminally. Do not lie, embellish, or attempt to conceal anything! Most background investigations will disclose negative and derogatory information during the process through responses by references and former employers, roommates and neighbors, and your answers to questions on the application, so be truthful and up-front from the start. If you're looking to hold a position of public trust and responsibility, you have to ask yourself why you would lie or conceal something to get the job in the first place. If during the course of the investigation, you are not being truthful, you can be certain your consideration for the position and being hired by the agency or company will be far more difficult to achieve.

While your personal history is a significant aspect of the background investigation, it is only one piece. Some candidates have an excellent employment history and family life, no criminal record, and a high credit score and academic achievement but still do not get hired, many times due to incomplete information, responses from references and others, and the inability to confirm and verify information and activities during periods of time lasting more than thirty days.

Detailed searches require a lot of time. It may take anywhere from 90 to 180 days to conduct and complete a search. The process involves many steps. First, the applicant is given a detailed questionnaire to complete. They have to provide a lot of information about themselves in that questionnaire and provide names and contacts of people who can verify the information. A thorough background check will involve interviewing friends, family, teachers, and employers. It is also likely you will be fingerprinted. Your fingerprints will match government and criminal records to you. Of course, searching those records takes time. Just remember to be patient since your patience throughout the process can be part of your consideration. The past of a person cannot guarantee his actions in the future, but the general thinking is that past actions are a good indicator of a person's character. A person with a clean past and good credit records is considered more likely to be an efficient and trustworthy employee. So much is the concern for security these days that such checks have become essential.

KNOWLEDGE POINT

A "profile" in a background check is a biographical account of your most noteworthy characteristics and achievements. These can be positive and negative. It is a collection of the characteristics that identify you. Profiles are used to help people who do not know you predict what kind of person you will be in the future, based on your past behavior.

Looking into your future with all the possibilities that you can explore and accomplish. *Qi Yang/Moment via Getty Images*

QUESTIONS TO CONSIDER

The last piece of this chapter is to get you acquainted with a background questionnaire. Answer the following questions. Be honest since nobody else will read the answers. When you are finished, consider what kind of person your answers described. Of course, that person is you, but pretend for a moment that you are reading this about someone else. Is this the sort of person you would trust with an important job? Investigators use questionnaires like this to create a profile of the person they are investigating. Investigators don't have the time or ability to get to know you as a person. They only get to know you through their investigation of your history. Your past actions count for everything.

Questions Regarding the Use of Illegal Drugs and/or Drug Activity

1. Have you ever used cannabis/marijuana?
2. In the past five years, have you used cannabis/marijuana?
3. Have you ever used any illegal drugs, including cannabis/marijuana?
4. Have you ever used any illegal drugs(s) or combination of illegal drugs other than marijuana?
5. Have you ever manufactured any illegal drugs?
6. Have you ever obtained, sold, distributed, or trafficked any illegal drugs?
7. Have you, in any of your travels outside the United States, used a substance legally in another country that would be considered an illegal substance in the United States?
8. Have you received drug counseling or rehabilitation while a student?

Questions Regarding the Use of Alcoholic Beverages

9. Do you ever drink alcoholic beverages like beer, wine, wine coolers, or liquor?
10. Do you remember how old you were the first time you drank alcohol, not counting sips you might have had as a child from an older person's drink?
11. How often do you drink alcohol? Daily? Weekly? Monthly?
12. Have you ever had five or more drinks of alcohol at a time?
13. As a student in junior high, high school, or college, have you done or experienced one or more of the following?

    a. had family issues or problems because of your use of alcohol beverages

    b. been absent from school because you used alcohol

    c. done poorly in school because you used alcohol

    d. been drunk while at school

    e. been drunk at a party or social event

    f. been a passenger in a vehicle in which the driver was under the influence of alcohol

    g. driven under the influence of alcohol

    h. been arrested because you used alcohol

    i. had an injury because you used alcohol

14. Do your parents permit you to drink alcohol in your home?

15. Do you discuss alcohol use with your parent(s)?

16. Do your parents know how much you drink?

17. Have your parents ever seen you drunk?

18. Do you have friends whose parents permit non–family members under the age of twenty-one to consume alcohol in their homes?

19. How many times in the past month or week has someone offered to give you, buy for you, or sell you alcohol?

20. Have you successfully used a fake ID to obtain alcohol?

21. Have you ever purchased alcohol without an ID?

22. As a young adult under the age of twenty-one, have you committed any of the following liquor law violations?

    a. citations for underage attempts to purchase

    b. citations for underage purchase

    c. citations for underage possession

    d. citations for underage consumption

    e. citations for underage possession or use of a fake ID

23. Which of the options below are accurate? Most people my age who drink, do so because of the following:

    a. They want to have a good time at a party.

    b. They are sad or depressed and want to feel better about themselves.

    c. They wish to rebel and defy their parents, teachers, or other adult authorities.

    d. They wish to fit in with or be accepted by their friends or peers.

24. As a young adult under the age of twenty-one, have you been involved in or committed any of the following offenses?

    a. property damage

    b. vandalism

    c. assault

    d. robbery

    e. murder

25. Are you a licensed driver who is under the age of twenty-one? Have you been involved in one of the following?

    a. zero tolerance citations

    b. underage DWI/DUI arrests

    c. underage DWI/DUI convictions

26. As a licensed driver who is under the age of twenty-one, have you been involved in one of the following?

    a. a motor vehicle alcohol-related crash

    b. a number of underage alcohol-related crashes

    c. motor vehicle alcohol-related injuries

    d. motor vehicle alcohol-related fatalities

27. As a licensed driver who is under the age of twenty-one, have you had your driver license suspended or revoked for underage consumption, purchase, or possession? Provide the number.

    a. number of license suspensions for alcohol-related motor vehicle offenses

    b. number of license revocations for alcohol-related motor vehicle offenses

28. Have you received any counseling/rehabilitation for alcohol abuse?

29. Do you think alcohol use by someone who is underage is:

    a. not a problem

    b. a minor problem

    c. a serious problem

30. Within the past year, do you think heavy use of alcohol among young adults your age has:
    a. increased
    b. decreased
    c. remained the same
31. In your opinion, who is responsible for contributing to the problem of alcohol use by youth under age twenty-one?

NOTE

1. Executive Order 10450, dating back to 1953, for a verification requirement for employees of the federal government.

2

How the Background Investigation Process Works

The moment you are considered for a position or program—whether it is a job in the private or government sector, college admission, a home loan, even a credit card application—that requires a background check, you will be given a form to fill out. You will need to fill it out completely and be entirely honest and as accurate as you can. That is the start of the background investigation process. Depending on what you are applying for, that may be all, or that may only be the beginning of a much longer process.

A background investigation includes a check of employment records, education records, interview of employment references (those you provide and others), neighborhood references (those you provide and others), and, in specific cases, family members. You will be requested to sign releases of information for credit records, medical records, and general information. Additional investigative checks may be requested or added as your investigation develops.

Depending on the sensitivity of the job or program, the investigation may include a check of your criminal history that covers the entire federal criminal database of the FBI, federal, state, county, and city court systems; state, county, and city law enforcement agencies throughout the United States; and even Interpol and other countries in the world that have an agreement with the United States.

When I was a kid, this didn't happen. What changed? Here's an example. According to a news report in 2018, a teacher working in a Georgia county public school system was arrested for impregnating a student in his class. As more information was made available to the public through police background checks, it was disclosed that the teacher had been arrested before for the same behavior in his previous employment with another school district in South Carolina.

According to information provided by the Georgia school district, the teacher's personnel file did not disclose any information related to his misconduct or being fired and arrested for his criminal actions while being employed by that school district. School districts are required to perform background checks on employees and volunteers, and these checks can take weeks. Even parents who volunteer for field trips are required to submit to a background check. Yet this teacher slipped through. Amazingly, there had been a longtime unwritten practice in the school district of letting problem employees resign in exchange for no adverse records placed on the file and no "bad references" when others inquire. What about the students in kindergarten, elementary, and middle school whom this person will now have access to see five days a week? Clearly, they were not considered by school officials. This is one recent example of why thorough background checks are needed for many jobs. In this case, the parents of the children in that school district have a right to know what sort of person teaches their children.

THE BACKGROUND CHECK PROCESS

When you submit to a background check, an investigator starts looking at your entire history. Not only is the investigator responsible for verifying all of the information you gave to them, but they will also dig up information, both good and bad, on you independently. The investigator will examine a sufficient period of your life to determine if you are an acceptable risk for the position for which you are applying.

Background investigators are required to identify, locate, and interview a number of people who know you well, including neighbors,

Contact and interaction with others through the process. *youak/DigitalVision Vectors via Getty Images*

friends, coworkers, supervisors, and sometimes even former spouses. You will be asked to name references whom the investigator can contact, but the investigator may also contact people you did not mention. Who and how many are interviewed is determined by the business, school, or government agency to which you are applying. The investigator wants to talk to as many knowledgeable people as possible to get a balanced, accurate, and comprehensive picture of you. Later, you may have an opportunity to refute any misleading or false information that was reported about you. Many types of background investigations involve a personal interview with you.

Before an investigation begins, *you* are required to verify:

- *Your US citizenship and the citizenship of immediate family members.* Verification is completed through your US birth certificate that is certified by your state of birth. For US citizens born outside the United States, a Consular Report of Birth Abroad or a State Department Form FS-545 or DS-1350 is used for verification. Additional forms include a Certificate of Birth, USCIS Form N-560 or N-561; Certificate of US Citizenship, USCIS Form 550 or 570; Naturalization Certificate; Permanent Resident Card, USCIS Form I-551; departure record with acceptable visa that authorizes employment in the United States, Form I-94; Employment Authorization Card, Form I-766; and Re-entry Permit, Form I-327.

- *Your date and place of birth.* Your date and place of birth are verified through your birth certificate maintained by the office of vital statistics in the state where your birth occurred. When you apply for a social security card and your driver's license, you must have your birth certificate to prove you are a US citizen.

- *Your education levels.* Verification of your level of education is completed through official transcripts from your high school and college or university. Your transcript confirms that you completed the required courses and graduated.

- *Your employment for the past seven or ten years.* Verification or your employment is completed through review of your employer's records, which will provide the confirmation of details such as dates, job title, salary, and eligibility for rehire. Many companies and institutions require an authorization for release of information from the current or former employee.

- *Your financial status (banking and other related income/expenses/ tax filings).* Confirmation and verification of your financial status is completed through review of credit reports, bank statements, and past tax filings.

- *Completion of any special government forms that might be appropriate.* The government requires that all applicants complete an authorization for release of information, a credit release form, and a medical release form in order to conduct the necessary background checks at law enforcement agencies, courts, medical institutions and counselors, financial institutions and agencies, as well as employers and rental properties and/or real estate–related companies.

The investigator will conduct federal, state, and local agency checks to review your criminal history within the jurisdictions where you have lived, worked, or attended school. Here are some things that an investigator will attempt to determine about you.

- *Sexual Behavior*—(1) Have you engaged in sexual behavior of a criminal nature, whether or not you have been prosecuted? (2) Have you demonstrated compulsive or addictive sexual behavior that indicated you were unable to stop a pattern of self-destructive or high-risk behavior or that may be symptomatic of a personality disorder? (3) Have you engaged in any sexual behavior that has caused/may cause you to be vulnerable to coercion, exploitation, or duress? (4) Have you engaged in sexual behavior of a public nature or that reflects a lack of discretion or judgment?
- *Personal Conduct*—(1) Have you refused to complete required security forms and releases and/or provide full and truthful answers to lawful questions of security officials, investigators, or other official representatives, in connection with a personnel security or trustworthiness determination? (2) Have you refused or failed without reasonable cause to undergo or cooperate with required security processing that may include medical and psychological testing? (3) Are you aware of any unfavorable information about you that could be provided by your friends, associates, neighbors, coworkers, and/or family?
- *Financial Considerations*—(1) Have you ever had financial problems with credit or creditors? (2) Do you have a history of not meeting financial obligations? (3) Are you able and willing to satisfy your debts? (4) Do you have any financial problems that are linked to gambling, drug abuse, alcoholism, or other issues of a security concern?
- *Alcohol Consumption*—(1) How do you describe your past and current use of alcoholic beverages: light, moderate—one to two drinks at home or social events? (2) Have you been involved in any alcohol-related incidents at home or work—with coworkers, friends, or family—disturbing the peace or any other criminal incidents related to alcohol use?

(3) Have you engaged in habitual or binge consumption of alcohol to the point of impaired judgment or blackout? (4) Have you been diagnosed by a credentialed medical professional (physician, clinical psychologist, or psychiatrist) of alcohol abuse or alcohol dependence?

- *Drug Involvement*—(1) Have you engaged in any improper or illegal involvement with drugs, to include the use of any illegal substance or the misuse of any prescription medication? (2) Have you tested positive for illegal use of drugs? (3) Have you ever used an illegal substance? (4) Do you intend to engage in illegal drug use or prescription drug abuse? (5) Have you possessed any drug, including cultivation, processing, manufacture, purchase, sale, or distribution, or drug paraphernalia?

- *Psychological Conditions*—(1) Have you been diagnosed by a credentialed mental health professional as having a condition that may indicate a defect in judgment, reliability, or stability? (2) Have you engaged in a pattern of high-risk, irresponsible, aggressive, anti-social, dysfunctional, paranoid, bizarre, or emotionally unstable behavior? (3) Have you taken prescription medication under the care of a physician for a mental health–related condition?

- *Criminal Conduct*—(1) Have you ever been involved in any allegations or admissions of criminal conduct regardless of whether or not you were formally charged or formally prosecuted? (2) Have you been accused of criminal conduct or made admissions of criminal conduct, regardless of whether you were formally charged? (3) Have you committed a serious crime or multiple lesser offenses? (4) Have you engaged in criminal activity that has gone undetected?

- *Handling of Protected Information*—(1) Have you ever been involved in the loading, downloading, drafting, editing, modifying, storing, transmitting, or otherwise handling of classified documents, data, etc.? (2) Have you been engaged in unauthorized disclosure of classified or other protected information to persons, including but not limited to business contacts, social media networks, conferences, or meeting attendees? (3) Have you ever been involved in any security incidents?

- *Outside Activities*—(1) Have you ever engaged in any service, whether compensated, volunteer, or employment, with a foreign country? (2) Have you engaged in similar service for a foreign national, organization, or other entity? (3) Have you engaged in any similar service for a representative of any foreign interest? (4) Have you ever failed to report or fully disclose any outside activity when required?
- *Use of Information Technology Systems*—(1) Do you comply with rules, procedures, guidelines, or regulations pertaining to information technology systems? (2) Have you ever illegally, or without authorization, entered into any information technology system or component thereof? (3) Have you ever illegally, or without authorization, modified, destroyed, or manipulated software, firmware, and hardware or denied other access to information residing on an information technology system?
- *Allegiance to the United States*—(1) Have you ever been involved in, supportive of, training to commit, or do you advocate any act of sabotage, espionage, treason, terrorism, sedition, or other act whose aim is to overthrow the government of the United States or alter the form of government by unconstitutional means? (2) Have you been associated or sympathized with persons who are attempting to commit, or who are committing, any of the above acts? (3) Have you been involved in activities that unlawfully advocate or practice the commission of acts of force or violence to prevent others from exercising their rights under the Constitution or laws of the United States or of any state?
- *Foreign Influence*—(1) Do you have any contact with any foreign family member (immediate or extended), business or professional associate(s), friend, or other person who is a citizen of or resident in a foreign country? (2) Do you have a connection to a foreign person, group, government, or country that creates a potential conflict of interest between your obligation to protect sensitive information or technology and your desire to help a foreign person, group, or country by providing that sensitive information or technology? (3) Is

everyone in your immediate family, including cohabitants and other persons to whom you are bound by affection, influence, or obligation, a citizen of the United States and *not* subject to any foreign influence? (4) Have you ever had a romantic involvement with a citizen of a foreign country? (5) Is there any conduct of yours that may make you vulnerable to coercion, exploitation, or pressure by a foreign country?

- *Foreign Preferences*—(1) Have you ever exercised any right, privilege, or obligation of foreign citizenship after becoming a US citizen or through the foreign citizenship of a family member? (2) As a result of your heritage or through the birth of your parents or grandparents, do you have the ability to apply for citizenship with another foreign country? (3) Are you currently exercising, or have you exercised in the past, dual/multi citizenship? (4) Have you ever possessed or used a foreign passport?

KNOWLEDGE POINT

During the investigative process, inappropriate conduct from your past may be uncovered. This is not automatic grounds for denying you your application. In fact, the investigators will look deeply into the actual incident and determine its relevance on a case-by-case basis.

Whatever the investigator uncovers about you that is troubling, they will consider the following factors:

- the nature, extent, and seriousness of the conduct;
- the circumstances surrounding the conduct, such as your knowledgeable participation;
- the frequency of the conduct and how recent it was;

- the extent to which participation was voluntary;
- the presence or absence of rehabilitation and other permanent behavioral changes;
- the motivation for the conduct;
- the potential for pressure, coercion, exploitation, or duress; and
- the likelihood of continuation or recurrence.

Each case must be judged on its own merits, and final determination remains the responsibility of the employer, school, or program to which you are applying.

WHO CONDUCTS BACKGROUND INVESTIGATIONS?

There are many companies that specialize in employment screening. I can't list them all by name, but the most important thing to keep in mind is that companies conducting background investigations fall into several broad categories. There are individuals, commonly known as "private investigators"; there are companies that do nothing but employment screening; and there are companies, called online data brokers, that scour the Internet for information on an individual.

KNOWLEDGE POINT

Businesses that employ large numbers of people may have an established relationship with a third-party background investigation company or may even use an affiliated company for their employment screening. Other background investigation companies may work on a less formal basis with employers. Some screening companies operate in specific areas of the country while others, including some private investigators, conduct background screenings nationwide.

As I have said before, you live in the information age. It is easy for employers to gather background information themselves. Much of it is computerized, allowing employers to log on to public records and commercial databases directly through dial-up networks or via the Internet. Finding one of these online companies is as easy as using an Internet search engine to find websites that specialize in "background checks."

FREQUENTLY ASKED QUESTIONS

Below are some frequently asked questions and answers from the US Office of Personnel Management regarding the background investigations process for employment opportunities.

I am being considered for a federal job and have been given a personnel security questionnaire. It's very long and asks a lot of personal questions. Do I have to answer all the questions on the form? Much of that information is already on my resume.

You must answer all of the questions on the form. The resume is part of the application process. The security questionnaire is part of the investigation process. All of the security questionnaire should be answered fully, accurately, and honestly.

What will happen if I refuse to give you some of this personal information?

The investigation is a job requirement. Providing the information is voluntary, but if you choose not to provide the required information, you will not meet the requirements of the job and will therefore not be considered further. If you are already employed by the federal government, your appointment will be terminated. The courts have upheld this principle.

What should I do if I remember something later, after I've filled out the form and returned it?

Immediately notify the security officials to whom you submitted the questionnaire.

I don't want everybody reading my personal information; who sees this information?

The only persons authorized to see your personal information are personnel security, suitability, and investigations professionals who have been investigated at the appropriate level and who have a genuine and demonstrated need to know for access to the information.

I'm not a criminal. Why do you want my fingerprints?

By checking the FBI's fingerprint files, we can verify your claim that you're not a criminal. Furthermore, Executive Order 10450 requires that all federal employees be fingerprinted.

My brother works for one of the largest companies in the world, but he didn't have to go through all this. Why should I?

Congress through statutes, the president through executive orders, and the agencies charged with carrying out these laws and orders have required this process. There is generally no requirement for private employers to use the same guidelines as public employers. Of course, if your brother's job with the private employer required him to have access to classified national security information as a contractor to the federal government, even your brother would have to be investigated.

Are you going to interview people other than those I name on the questionnaire? If so, why?

Yes. Background investigators are required to identify, locate, and interview a sufficient number of people who know you well. We want a balanced and unbiased investigation. It would be a questionable investigative practice to only interview persons whom the individual being investigated identified for us.

Is it okay if I guess at dates and addresses that I barely remember?

Providing information that is as complete and accurate as possible will assure that your investigation is completed in an efficient and timely manner. If you are unable to answer a question with precision, provide approximate information and note that you have done so on the questionnaire. If you are interviewed in person, point out the approximated information on the questionnaire to the investigator.

Why do you need information about my relatives?

Relatives sometimes influence the actions of family members. We need to determine whether you could be exploited by threats or pressure against your relatives or if they themselves could exert pressure against you.

Will I get a chance to explain some of the answers I provide?

Yes. Many types of background investigations involve a personal interview. Moreover, you may submit information on extra pages with your questionnaire if you feel you need to explain more fully details or circumstances of the answers you put on the form.

What if you talk to someone who just doesn't like me and they lie about me?

We talk to as many knowledgeable people as possible to get a balanced, accurate, and comprehensive picture of the person being investigated. Later, you may have an opportunity to refute any misleading or false information that was reported about you.

I was cited for speeding once. Will that keep me from getting a job or a clearance?

Not necessarily. Any negative information is evaluated regarding how recently it occurred, its seriousness, its relevance to the position and duties, and in light of, and in relationship to, all other information about you.

I was arrested for shoplifting ten years ago. Is that going to be held against me now?

Not necessarily. Any negative information is evaluated regarding how recently it occurred, its seriousness, its relevance to the position and duties, and in light of, and in relationship to, all other information about you.

I have a physical disability. Will that hurt my chances for a job?

No. It is against federal law to discriminate against an individual based on his or her disability.

Are you going to tell my supervisor that I'm looking for a job?

It is a requirement of a background investigation, and actual employment, that your current employer be contacted. We must verify your employment data and make other inquiries concerning your background. If you are a federal employee or contractor, for example, it may be that your current employer needs you to have a security clearance for the work you do. In other instances, you are asked to complete the investigative form for an investigation and clearance only after a conditional offer of employment has been made for a position requiring a security clearance.

Who decides whether I get the job or a security clearance?

Officials at the agency requiring the investigation will evaluate your case and communicate their recommendation to the appropriate personnel or security office.

Is it true that the investigation will include a credit report about me?

Yes. A search of the records of commercial credit reporting agencies is an integral part of almost all background investigations.

Do you ever interview someone's ex-spouse or relatives?

Yes, although, in many instances, interviewing ex-spouses or relatives is not mandatory.

Why is detailed information about my education required?

Educational history is necessary for jobs that require specific education and expertise. Any information supplied by the applicant must be verified.

I was politically active during the last elections. Will that hurt my chances for a job or a clearance?

No. It will neither hurt nor help your chances.

Do I have to go to a police station to be fingerprinted?

You may go to a police station to be fingerprinted. In most instances, however, the agency requiring the investigation and clearance will fingerprint you.

Doesn't the FBI conduct all federal background investigations?

The US Office of Personnel Management, the Department of Defense, and a few other agencies share this responsibility. The FBI mostly conducts investigations on the following: high-level presidential appointees, cabinet officers, agency heads, and staff who may work at the White House directly for the president. Also, companies such as Omniplex, CACI, and Key Point are contracted to provide background investigations for the Department of Defense, Homeland Security, and other agencies and departments within the government.

Why do the government or contractor companies (such as Omniplex, Key Point, or CACI) investigate federal applicants, employees, and contractors?

The interests of national security require that all persons privileged to be employed in the departments and agencies of the government shall be reliable, trustworthy, of good conduct and character, and of complete and unswerving loyalty to the United States. This means that the appointment of each civilian employee in any department or agency of the government is subject to investigation. The scope of the investigation will vary, depending on the nature of the position and the degree of harm that an individual in that position could cause.

The requirement to be investigated applies whether or not the position requires a security clearance (in order to have access to classified national security information).

How can I see the report you prepare about me?

The only persons authorized to see this information are personnel security, suitability, and investigations professionals who have been investigated and have a demonstrated need to review the information. You may request a copy of your investigation file under provisions of the Privacy Act. You will have to contact the agency or department for information on requesting your completed background investigation report. You must include your full name, Social Security number, and date and place of birth, and you must sign your request.

WHY IS ALL OF THIS NECESSARY?

If you are reading and thinking about background checks for the first time, it may seem very intimidating. You may be wondering why all of the digging into your past is necessary. It may even seem unfair that someone is being hired to discover every bad or illegal thing you ever did, write it in a report, and show it to other people, just so you can get into a new school or get a job. Consider what it's like to be on the other side, however. You know among your friends whom you can trust the most, whom you can rely on for certain things and whom you can rely on for others. You have known your friends for a long time, and your knowledge of what kind of people they are comes from that. A potential employer or a college admissions counselor receives many applications and doesn't have the luxury of spending years getting to know each person. They must base their decision whether you are right for a school or a job on information from the application, and part of the application is the background check. That background check builds a picture of you based on all of your recorded history as either reliable and trustworthy or unreliable and untrustworthy.

What does that picture say? Nobody is perfect. Every single person has at least one thing in their past that they regret. Therefore, if your past has a few spots that you think look bad, you are not alone. How bad are those spots? That depends on how you handled them or continue to handle them. Kids do all sorts of things, and they learn by doing. Teenagers are allowed to be teenagers. The problems arise when you are an adult and still doing childish things or, worse, if you are a teenager but getting into adult trouble. Those are the things you want to avoid because those are the things that will create red flags on your background investigation report. The background investigation process looks at patterns of behavior and not at any single action or incident. The investigation is trying to present you as a "whole" person, which includes your strengths as well as your weaknesses. Keep moving forward and expect the best of yourself in life in all that you do!

After taking the time to read this chapter, I would like for you to ask yourself: What are my concerns regarding the background investigation process as it pertains to my past and what is my current situation and future moving forward?

QUESTIONS TO CONSIDER

1. What are some of my concerns about my history?
2. Do I have secrets in my past that could cause problems for my future career/job market?
3. Am I aware of some of the personal questions I will have to answer on my application for consideration of employment opportunities?
4. How should I prepare for the investigative inquiry/background check/questionnaire?
5. What have I done and am I doing to make necessary changes in my life to address potential problems in the investigative process?
6. What type of person am I with regard to understanding and following the guidelines, laws, and rules of society?

3

You, the Internet, and Social Media

Whether you know it or not, whether you like it or not, almost everything you do is creating a history for other people to read. This includes obvious things, like posting on social media. It can include less obvious things, like sneaking out with your friends to have a beer or smoke some weed. Some of you might ask, "How can other people find out about me drinking if I don't get caught?" Well, can you be sure you will not get caught? Plenty of people find themselves in a bad situation because they thought they were being careful but things unexpectedly went wrong. We live in the "age of information." That means that we are recorded and tracked more than at any previous point in history. Security cameras are cheap, and they are everywhere. If your cell phone has a signal, you can communicate with people around the globe, but that same tiny phone serves as a homing beacon because your service provider knows exactly where you are! Satellites in space can take pictures of the license plate on a car. What is more, all of this information is permanent and easy to access. The question you should ask yourself every day is: What am I doing now that could come back to haunt me later?

With respect to social media, the answer to that previous question is probably, "A lot!" It may seem harmless to post things on social media, but time has demonstrated that stuff on the Internet does not go away. It is strange to think of the Internet as permanent, but it practically is.

Therefore, you should think before you post. Posting on social media can cause irreparable harm to your reputation or the reputation of others. Posts on social media have been used to bar applicants from getting into college, from getting jobs, and from getting security clearances, and they have been used against persons in courts of law.

There was a young woman selected for the prestigious honor of working as a summer intern at a US embassy in a foreign country. In the security briefing that she received before taking this position, she was told *not* to take pictures of anyone or anything at the embassy and never to post any information about her position at the embassy on social media. Within the first week, she took pictures of herself outside of the embassy and posted it to Facebook stating, "Look where I am!" Within another week, she was removed from her position at the embassy, she was sent back to the United States, her security clearance was taken away from her, and she was flagged in the security clearance system as never to have a clearance with the Department of State again due to a security violation. Not only did she commit a security violation by posting pictures on social media, but she may also have compromised the cover of agents of the federal government placed in secure locations. How is that possible? Embedded within the pixels of digital photography are the time and location the picture was taken. You may not see it or know it is there, but once it is posted, that information can be hacked.

Perhaps a more famous example of someone suffering for social media posts is Michael Phelps, the Olympic swimmer. He lost millions of dollars in endorsements from the posting on social media where he was smoking drugs at a party after he won his Olympic gold medals.

What are the lessons here? Do not ever put anything in writing (or in pictures) that can be used against you. Do not take compromising pictures of yourself or let others take compromising pictures of you. Finally, do not put anything on social media that could come back to haunt you later because it will.

The following are some facts and statistics regarding young people's use of social media. These come from the Pew Research Center Internet and Technology Study, March 2018. According to the researchers, both government and educational, about 88 percent of teenagers in the United States, ages thirteen to seventeen, have access to a desktop or laptop computer through home or school. Researchers report that about 74 percent of girls and 71 percent of boys have access to a smartphone, and 62 percent of girls and 54 percent of boys have access to a tablet. Most teenagers have access to the Internet and social media on a device that is inexpensive, weighs a few ounces, and fits easily in your pocket. When I was growing up, only the very wealthy had mobile phones, they weighed several pounds, and they were so large they had to be carried in briefcases. Accessibility has increased dramatically in several decades and is now completely accepted as normal.

Young people connected in today's social media network. *Orbon Alija/E+ via Getty Images*

FACEBOOK

According to founder Mark Zuckerberg, Facebook was created with the mission to "give people the power to share the world more open and connected." Today, people use Facebook to stay connected with family, friends, and employers and to discover what is going on around the world. The following are some Facebook statistics (according to Facebook) you should know:

- Active users worldwide number 2.17 billion (the most widely used social platform in the world).
- The average number of friends for Facebook users is 155 (but users would trust only four of them).
- Seventy-nine percent of Americans use Facebook (Instagram is second with 32 percent).
- Twenty-eight percent is the average of their Facebook friends they consider to be genuine or close friends.
- Eighty-three percent of parents with a teen between the ages of thirteen and seventeen are friends with their child on Facebook.
- Thirty-nine percent of Facebook users say they are connected to people they have never met in person.

Here are some teen-specific statistics:

- Ninety-three percent of all teen Facebook users provide their real name.
- Ninety-two percent include profile pictures of themselves.
- Eighty-five percent list interests in books, movies, and music.
- Eighty-three percent include their actual birthday.
- Seventy-three percent include their school name on their profile.
- Seventy-two percent list the city and state where they live.
- Sixty-three percent post their relationship status.
- Fifty-four percent list their e-mail address.
- Twenty-five percent post videos of themselves.
- Twenty-one percent include personal telephone numbers.

These statistics are shocking and surprising and should serve as warning signs to all Facebook users. Think of all the personal information that is being voluntarily revealed. The more you reveal, the more easily you are targeted by predators, identity thieves, and other "bad" people. In addition, college admissions officers and potential employers search Facebook profiles to learn more about prospective candidates, and if they do not like what they see, they do not have to admit you or hire you.

Be aware of Facebook privacy settings and use them! Keep your personal information private. Keep your posts private. Even when you share with friends, they may share with those you do not expect or intend to see it. You disclose information at your own risk and with a limited feeling and knowledge of complete privacy from Facebook and all online social media. If you do not know a lot about basic safety and security online, ask family and friends who do or people at your school.

INSTAGRAM

Instagram was created in 2010 as a photo- and video-sharing network, and it is owned by Facebook as of April 2012. Through Instagram, users can take photos, apply a filter, and then share these photos on the service or a variety of other social networking services including Facebook, Twitter, and Tumblr. Like with Facebook, you can have your profile open to public view so that all users can see your posts, or you can set it to private and then users need to request your approval before following you and seeing all your posts. Many of those who have Instagram profiles may use this social networking site as a "challenge" to post the most pictures, have the most followers, and of course receive the most likes and (positive) comments. Some research has shown that students can become addicted to posting pictures and post without thinking about the post itself and who will see it. Also, young users may have access to inappropriate content.

Here are some statistics you should know about Instagram users from Instagram (2017–2018):

- Sixty-eight percent of users are female.
- Thirty-one percent of American women and 24 percent of men use Instagram.
- Thirty-two percent of all Internet users are on Instagram.
- Active monthly users number one billion.
- Active daily users number five hundred million.
- Daily stories users number four hundred million.
- Eighty percent of users are located outside the United States.
- The number of accounts a user can have is five.
- The amount of time for videos is two to sixty seconds.
- A user can group message fifteen people.
- Sixty-three percent of Internet users aged thirteen to seventeen use Instagram daily.
- Sixty-four percent of college students consider Instagram the most narcissistic social media service.

Women are twice as likely to use Instagram as men, and they are more vulnerable in society than men. If you are a young woman reading this who uses Instagram, be aware! Above and beyond having your posts read by prospective employers, you could be targeted by people with genuinely bad intentions. Keep your posts private. Search regularly to see whether other people are sharing posts by or about you without your knowledge. These things can affect your present and your future.

SNAPCHAT

Snapchat was created for mobile devices that allow subscribers to send photos to other subscribers. Snapchat allows users to set a one- to ten-second expiration of the photo. Users can send time-limited photos that might be embarrassing or just funny without a significant fear that it will find its way to other social media sites where it might exist forever.

TWITTER

Twitter was created as a social networking service that enables users to send short (280-character) messages called "tweets." According to the latest social media industry figures, Twitter currently ranks as one of the top social networks worldwide based on "active" users. Twitter reports that as of 2018, Twitter had more than 335 million monthly active users. Registered users can read and post tweets as well as follow other users via updated feed. According to Twitter, the most-followed celebrity on Twitter is Katy Perry, with more than 107 million followers.

According to researchers, Twitter is being used by teenagers as a source for news and events of interest to them. Twitter, like Snapchat and Instagram, offers the speed and accessibility for news to break quickly. On the other hand, Twitter users can post information and images without any verification or fact-checking. Twitter is, therefore, as much a source of lies, propaganda, rumors, and speculation as of genuine news.

While conducting research regarding Twitter and teenage users, I found one disturbing way that a subculture of young people is boosting their profiles. Young people who have been arrested are posting their mugshots along with stories of their altercations with law enforcement. Their followers encourage this behavior by rating the "worst" stories as the "best." This particularly applies to young women who gain reputations as "baddies." Even if this seems cool to you right now as a young reader, I promise you that it will not be cool in a few years. If you were to participate in behavior like this, it would have a negative impact on your future the moment you became an adult.

In October of 2018, *Time* magazine published a story that indicated there is a correlation between the amount of time people spend reading computer screens (phones and laptops) and clinical diagnoses of depression and anxiety. In short, the more you are on your phone, the more likely you are to be depressed. The same article, which is not the only article on the subject and which cites many studies, indicated that the more time you spend on your phone, the more likely you are to be distracted, emotionally unstable, unable to make friends, and unable to finish tasks.

According to researchers who have studied teens and social media, over 80 percent of American youths use their mobile phones for texting, e-mail, and mobile Internet access. Also, researchers have found that middle school, high school, and college students use Facebook several times per day, every day, to communicate with their friends and family. The most obvious negative aspect of social media networking is the loss of "face-to-face" interaction with your friends and other people. Some young people claim they feel more comfortable with "virtual" friends than with real friends and that they find it easier to talk or chat with others through social media due to their lack of communication skills. By communicating through social media, you are missing out on the development of critical social skills. Through your communications by social media, you are missing the opportunity to "see and read" body language, facial expressions, and vocal inflections from the others. Why is that important? According to two studies on communication by Albert Mehrabian in 1967, when trying to communicate feelings, opinions, and attitudes, only 7 percent of the actual message is through words; 38 percent is conveyed by tone, and 55 percent is conveyed by body language. If you do not know how to read a person's tone and body language, you are missing 93 percent of what they are saying, if they are talking about their feelings or attitudes! When we talk to our friends, family, even work colleagues, it is rarely about just passing factual information. Usually, we are talking about feelings and attitudes.

This disconnect from personal interactions is believed by researchers to be part of the rise of cyberbullying because the bullies do not have to deal with the reactions of their victims. The bullies are naturally isolated by virtue of social media. Of course, avoiding consequences makes it easier to do anything. The results of many cases of cyberbullying reveal the majority of harassers to be friends or acquaintances. They simply found it easy to be mean online. Related to this, studies have revealed that people are more likely to "like" a post or photo that received many "likes" already from those in their network (this can include bullying posts). This action may be a way of "conforming" to the favor of others on the Internet so there is less perceived "pressure" on the individual user. I will talk about cyberbullying again in the next chapter.

How can social media affect your education or career? In 2017, Harvard rescinded admission to ten students who had already received letters of admission for posting obscene and racist material on social media, which included jokes about the Holocaust and abusing children. In 2019, Harvard rescinded admission to Kyle Kashuv, a survivor of the

Privacy concerns and issues are "real" and require security to protect our social media interactions. *Leafedge/Digital Vision Vectors via Getty Images*

2018 murders at Stoneman Douglas High School, who became famous for his pro-gun tweets. It was not those specific tweets but rather racist tweets he made when he was sixteen that caused Harvard to revoke his admission. Recognize that private schools and employers do not owe you admission or employment. If they find anything that can cause them to consider you a bad fit, they will simply not hire or admit you. Furthermore, if you are already admitted or employed, it is "at will," and you can be expelled or revoked when bad behavior comes to light. According to a 2018 CareerBuilder survey, 70 percent of employers screen candidates using social media. Perhaps more importantly, 34 percent *continue to screen employees* on social media as long as they are employed.

SECURING YOUR SOCIAL MEDIA

Reports from companies that study these things, companies like Norton, PC World, and Ever FI, indicate that more than 79 percent of the US population is active on social networks, but more than half of those people have no idea how to stay safe on social media. Users openly share data or use poorly protected passwords that can be broken by good guessing. Each year millions of users are the victim of social media account hacks. This means that they have personal information stolen or fall prey to online scams.

Learning how to stay safe on social media is especially important with the increasing prevalence of integrated payment systems and apps, phone verification, and touch technology. When someone steals an account, they likely have access to bank or credit card information, home or work addresses, and other very personal information that could be used to steal the victim's identity.

Use Privacy and Security Settings to Protect Your Information

You should always use the highest security settings. Make sure that information is only shared with people you know well. Best of all, do

KNOWLEDGE POINT

Identity theft is very serious. It means that a person has stolen the information that identifies you as you—information such as your Social Security number or credit card number and the security code—and committed acts in your name, without your knowledge or consent. Why is this so important? Imagine someone commits a crime claiming to be you and has all of the documentation to demonstrate that it is you. How do you prove that it wasn't you? The process can sometimes take years and cause considerable stress. According to a study by the US House of Representatives Ways and Means Committee in 2018, sixty million Americans had their identities stolen.

not post anything anywhere that could be used against you or used to impersonate you. Make sure your passwords are strong. Do not use simple words or things that people who know you could easily guess. Never use a password that a total stranger could guess, for example the word "password" or the number sequence "12345." If two-factor authentication is available for a password, use it. Two-factor authentication means that, in addition to providing a password, you must answer predetermined questions to which only you know the answer or you must respond to an e-mail or text on a separate device.

Facebook has sophisticated safety measures that let you control who can see your profile. Rather than sharing information with everyone, you should limit your account to very close friends. To avoid becoming the victim of social media phishing and social media scams, never share personal information that can be used to target you, such as:

- information regarding location,
- home or work addresses,
- phone numbers and e-mails, and
- birth date and other private information.

Information about your hometown, parents' and grandparents' last names, maiden name, and birth date can be used to answer privacy questions on bank financial platforms and other websites. If the information is not kept private, you are vulnerable. Also, if you see that a friend is sharing their information, tell them not to.

Strong Passwords and Secure Accounts

Strong passwords will protect your online accounts from being hacked, which helps a great deal in terms of identity theft, social media scams, and account takeovers. Here are some tips for a good password:

- Use a unique mix of letters, numbers, and signs.
- Have at least ten characters.
- Change your password every six months.

Use a different password on each of your accounts to ensure that if someone gets into one, they do not have access to all of them. If you have many different accounts, each with a separate strong password, you may want to consider using a password manager. A password manager is an app that handles all of your passwords, so you do not have to remember them. Instead, you log into the password manager, and the password manager logs you into your various accounts. It keeps track of your passwords, and it is encrypted. You only need to remember one password, that of the manager. Of course, you must make sure that that password is extremely strong since it is the master key that opens all of your accounts.

Manage Your Friends and Followers

Everyone receives friend and follower requests, but you should be careful of whom you accept. It may seem great to have thousands of friends on Facebook, but unless you can actually claim those people as friends in real life, friends that you know and trust, you could be leaving yourself vulnerable to scams and identity theft. Do not accept a friend request just because. Be wary of the following:

- accounts with no information;
- accounts with only a few friends (real people start with their real friends, not strangers);
- accounts that immediately start sending you messages with no real purpose, especially in broken English; and
- accounts that start sending you links, promising things, asking for investment, or promising love.

Even though many social media platforms are working to ensure the security of their users, do not assume that that is enough. You must also work to keep your account secure and private.

Watch Out for Social Media Scams and Phishing

Social media scams and social media phishing are two of the most common problems on social media platforms today. The links used for these types of attacks normally attempt to steal either your identity or your money or they work to spread a bot or virus to your network of friends. Watch out for the following:

- chain letters;
- urgent request for money;
- links to quizzes and games that require your phone number or bank details first;
- links to photos and click-bait article titles that take you off the network;

- shortened URLs, which can be used to hide malware and viruses on a link;
- schemes to make you rich after you pay a fee;
- sweepstakes and lottery winnings; and
- sudden romantic interests asking for money.

Some of these social media scams are harmless, but others can steal a great deal of information or money from you. Never give away personal or financial information on social media.

Research Everything Before You Click and Share Data

To be sure you are staying safe on social media, do your homework before accepting, clicking, or sharing digital content. This means paying attention to what is being sent to you and what you are sharing. For example, if a friend asks you for money under suspicious circumstances, you could follow through on this by calling them to ask about their request. If a friend you thought was already a Facebook connection adds you, you could call them to ask about it. Similarly, if you see an astounding bit of news from a website you do not know, it is almost always better to look it up through your own Google search instead of clicking on a link. If you are being prompted to fill in data for a quiz, you could look up the quiz and see whether it is reliable (or better yet never give information to a quiz app). This little bit of extra effort will help prevent potential hacking, spamming, or phishing issues.

CLEANING UP YOUR SOCIAL MEDIA ACCOUNTS

Beyond updating your privacy setting and watching out for scams and unwanted posts, there are other things you can do to help clean up your social media accounts.

Review and Clear Out Your Friend List and Contacts

Over the years, most people can say that they have racked up hundreds of old friends, coworkers, and acquaintances on Facebook and other social media apps, not to mention public page likes. Having such a large network of social media "friends" with people you barely know and tons of public pages sharing new updates all the time gives you less control over what is posted and shared on your feed. A great rule to remember is to go through your friend list maybe once a year and unfriend anybody you have not made contact with in more than a year, with the exception of family members and special friends who live across the country or overseas. You can cut down the lost connections on your list this way and avoid getting caught up in the lives of people from your past.

"Unlike" All Those Pages You Don't Need

As far as liked pages go, ditch the ones you could live without and keep the ones you actually enjoy checking up on or that are extremely useful to you. Go to Facebook.com/pages and check the "Liked Pages" to see a grid of all the pages you have liked so you can work your way through unliking the ones you need to get rid of. Remember that you can also customize your news feed so that you can hide or snooze post updates from certain pages and people without unliking or unfriending them.

Remove Old Third-Party Apps

While you are on cleanup duty, you might as well delete unwanted third-party apps you have installed over the years; they may not be a distraction, but deleting them can certainly help to protect your privacy.

Review Your Social Media Accounts

You are responsible for reviewing your news on social media! This requires commonsense instincts. Social media activities require critical thinking, research, and reading between the lines. It is important not to believe everything you read. Through the background investigations process, you have to review all your social media profiles, such as Facebook, Instagram, and Twitter, on a regular basis. It is your responsibility to make sure your profiles are private, as you do not want others (especially investigators) to see anything that could/would be embarrassing to you and change the way people see who you are. Consider the following as you review your accounts:

1. What social media headline are you most interested in?
2. Who are the social media authors and contributors on the post subject/topic?
3. What is the history of the authors and contributors regarding the post subject/topic? How do you know?
4. What and who are the source of the social media post?
5. Is the source of the social media post known? Are they reliable? How do you know?
6. Why are you a part of the target audience? Is it because of your age? Your gender? Your posts on the subject?
7. What post appeals to you the most? Why?
8. Why do you post comments or repost comments māde by specific individuals?
9. Do you post photos that may not be appropriate to be viewed by anyone?
10. Does the post appear to be biased or misleading?
11. How can you validate the social media posts that interest you?
12. How do these posts affect your personal views or interests?
13. Could the post be considered offensive?
14. What are your concerns regarding some of your posts in the past?
15. Are you making the necessary review, changes, and corrections related to all your social media connections?

THE BOTTOM LINE

The Internet can be a dangerous place—and social media is no exception—but it does not have to be. Taking the time to protect your data and to use the security tools provided to you by the app to control how and where you share data is the best way to protect yourself online. You should also review your social media accounts periodically, change passwords, and review any apps or plugins that have access to your account, so you can maintain long-term security. Since social media is part of our daily lives and likely to remain so for an exceptionally long time, it is important to use it safely and securely.

What should you take away from this information about social media and your future? I hope you recognize that it is extremely easy to reveal too much about your life. Therefore, you should be extra careful when posting to social media to make sure that the privacy settings are on the most secure options. Even then, you should not post anything to social media that you would not want someone to find in the future, either by accident or because of a thorough investigation.

Your future opportunities are connected to your decisions of today. Do not allow your social media connections and involvement to prevent you from reaching your future goals and objectives in life.

Communications and interactions in today's world. *bubaone/DigitalVision Vectors via Getty Images*

QUESTIONS TO CONSIDER

The following are some questions to help you think about how your personal use of social media and the Internet might have affected or will affect an investigation into your background:

1. Why do I use social media? What are my reasons and true interest in being a part of social media today?
2. What apps do I use?
3. Why do I use these apps?
4. Do I have to be on every social media network? If so, why?
5. What type of content should I share? What concerns should I have about the content I am sharing if it is being viewed by many people across the globe?
6. What is my favorite thing about being on social media? How important are the "likes" I receive from others on social media?
7. What is the worst thing about social media? Am I a part of the "best" or "worst" part of my social media network?
8. Who am I connected to on social media? How much do I really know about the people on my social media network?
9. How does social media affect my time? How much time am I spending on social media (daily, weekly, and/or monthly)?
10. How does social media affect my friendships? Who are my friends?
11. How does social media affect my reputation? Am I going in the "right" direction for me through my social media network?
12. How does social media networking affect my privacy? Is my social media life private or public?

4

Life Challenges
What You Should Know

What is it that you want to do with your life? What do you want to be when you're older? Whatever it is, remember that the choices you make when you're young can have a serious effect on what you want to do later. We all have to make choices and live with the consequences. In this guide, I will discuss choices that you may find yourself facing as high school students and how these choices can affect your ability to pass a background check in the not-so-far future. A friend and federal investigator for thirty-eight years shared this story. For twenty years, I conducted background investigations for the Department of Defense, the Peace Corps, the Office of Personnel Management, and the Department of State. There are many ways you can make really bad choices and ruin your prospects for the future. In this chapter, I am going to tell you some stories from my days as an investigator. Of course, the names are made up, but the events are real.

Kyle was seventeen years old when he was out with friends driving on a main highway near Washington, D.C. They saw some other friends on the road and began racing their cars. The young man lost control of his car and ran head-on into oncoming traffic. The other driver was killed. Everyone would agree that this is a horrible accident, but even accidents have consequences. It's probably true that, had Kyle not been speeding, he would not have lost control of the car, causing the accident.

Instead, he was arrested and charged with vehicular homicide. What's more, he was tried as an adult, even though he was only seventeen. In most states, even a fourteen-year-old can be tried as an adult for a criminal offense. The young man was tried, found guilty, and sentenced to five years in jail and a $10,000 fine.

KNOWLEDGE POINT

Usually, when persons below the age of eighteen are charged with a crime, they are tried in a separate court reserved for other minors. But every state allows for minors to be tried as adults under certain circumstances: (1) the nature of the crime is extremely serious, (2) the juvenile perpetrator understood the serious nature of the crime and its consequences, (3) the offender has a history of similar crimes, and/or (4) the offender has been tried as an adult before. If you are under the age of eighteen and you commit a crime, don't think your age will automatically lead to lesser punishment.

Several years ago, my daughter's friend was involved in an unfortunate incident. Both my daughter and her friend are women in their early twenties. The friend was driving her car in Washington, D.C. She had an air freshener hanging from the rearview mirror in her car. She didn't know it, but this is illegal in D.C. A police officer pulled her over and asked to see her driver's license, registration, and cell phone. The young lady complied, and the officer found some texts related to marijuana use on her cell phone. This gave him probable cause to search her car, where he found a very small amount of marijuana and a drug pipe. The young lady was arrested on a possession charge. She didn't know that a hanging air freshener was illegal. She probably didn't think about the marijuana and pipe since they were packed away and hidden. She probably thought she was doing the right thing by complying with all that the officer had asked her to do, including giving him her phone. One unexpected thing led to another. Now, even if this young lady is able to get the charge dismissed, it will forever be on her record as an *arrest* and may affect her future employment options. Why? Because many background checks ask, "Have you ever been *arrested*?" not "Have you ever been *charged*?"

Know the traffic laws and obey them. Little violations can lead to big problems. Be aware that background checks are interested in any fine over $300. Repeated traffic fines show a lack of respect for rules and regulations and can impact your ability to obtain a job. You could also end up in court and even serve jail time.

Drinking alcohol has been part of American culture, and its use by young people has been accepted by many as part of growing up. In fact, during the late 1960s and early 1970s, many states lowered the legal drinking age from twenty-one to eighteen. Following this change, the number of alcohol-related traffic fatalities among people in that age range increased remarkably. Beginning in the early 1980s, some states increased the drinking age to twenty-one again, but not all states did.

Evon lives on suburban Long Island, New York, where she attends a high school with more than one thousand students. She comes from a conservative and strict upbringing, as do several of her classmates and friends. Evon is a pretty normal kid, but it's noteworthy that she had never tried alcohol or drugs and never broken the law. In honor of her upcoming high school graduation, she and a few friends decided that they were going to try marijuana and drink until they were drunk. They carefully planned this for when Evon's parents were away and they could be in her house without supervision. It was a "success," in that she got very drunk, to the point of passing out, and high. But it led to further consequences that she couldn't see at the time.

KNOWLEDGE POINT

(NATIONAL INSTITUTE OF HEALTH RESEARCH STUDIES)

Back in 1984, because of the lack of consistent drinking age laws from state to state, the federal government got involved. Congress passed legislation that would withhold federal highway construction funds from any state that had not raised the legal drinking age to twenty-one. By 1988, all states had adopted twenty-one as the minimum legal drinking age. If you ever wondered why you aren't allowed to buy alcohol until years after you are allowed to drive, vote, get married, and join the military, it's because an entire generation of young people demonstrated that they couldn't drink responsibly. If anything demonstrates that choices have consequences, that does.

Based on her first experience with alcohol and drugs, Evon became a little more cavalier about using them. Sometimes it's fascinating to see how one experience can change a person's behavior dramatically. Evon had never used or drank before, but once she tried, she started using and drinking regularly. In fact, she tried them a few more times, and on the third time, she and her friends went into a clothing store and tried to steal some merchandise. I say tried because she was recorded by the store's security cameras. The police were called, and Evon was arrested.

Evon's parents bailed her out, but no secret was made of her arrest among her family and friends. Prior to graduation from high school, Evon had received and accepted a scholarship to one of the best universities in the country. The university application included questions that specifically asked about any use of illegal substances and unlawful or criminal acts. At the time, Evon answered "no," a truthful answer, but the application also required that applicants update the university if that were to change. Evon chose not to let the school know about her arrest, and the university did not follow up. She seems to have skirted a problem with the school but not really. Her arrest is public record, and any serious background investigation can find it. It will reveal that she was arrested for theft while under the influence of drugs. It will also reveal that she chose to hide it from her school. This is a compounding

KNOWLEDGE POINT

(UNIFORM DRINKING ACT OF 1984 OF THE U.S. CONGRESS)

According to the Center for Disease Control, alcohol is the most commonly used and abused drug among youth in the United States.

- Excessive drinking is responsible for more than 4,300 deaths among underage youth each year and cost the United States $24 billion in 2010.

- Although drinking by persons under the age of twenty-one is illegal, people aged twelve to twenty years drink 11 percent of all alcohol consumed in the United States. More than 90 percent of this alcohol is consumed in the form of binge drinking.

- On average, underage drinkers consume more drinks per drinking occasion than adult drinkers.

- In 2013, there were approximately 119,000 emergency-room visits by persons aged twelve to twenty-one for injuries and other conditions linked to alcohol.

problem. She lied about her past. Since she got away with it the first time, she may not consider the consequences of trying to hide it on future applications. If it is ever discovered, it will be the arrest, the drug use, and a series of lies to hide it. Of course, I'm not condemning Evon's motivation for trying to hide the arrest. It's probably very embarrassing, and something she has sworn to herself never to repeat. She probably thinks that if she doesn't talk about it and is a good student and citizen the rest of her life, it will simply be a thing of the past. That may be true, but Evon isn't the only person to know about this incident. Her friends and family know, also. They could, accidentally or on purpose, reveal this in the future, or it may be discovered by a more diligent background check; either way, it will require some serious explaining.

I was involved in an investigation of a California high school student I'll call Brian who was interested in joining the Army. This story is educational not only because of Brian's choices but because of those whom he trusted for advice. Brian wanted to be an Army officer and investigated the ROTC (Reserve Officers' Training Crops) program in his junior year. He developed a relationship with the recruiter over the course of his senior year, and he was encouraged to keep his grades up, volunteer in his community, and in other ways satisfy the entrance requirements for an officer in the Army.

When you join the military through a program like ROTC, even if you are initially accepted, it is conditional. That means they have the right to remove you from the program later if you fail to maintain their standards or if they discover something troubling about your past. Furthermore, everyone who applies for a government job (not just the military) must go through a background check. For the military, it is extensive. To be considered for the military, you must sign a waiver giving investigators permission to examine everything in your past: your credit history and your financial standing, your education and employment history, and your criminal history, if you have one. Furthermore, they interview your neighbors, colleagues, friends, and family to determine your character.

KNOWLEDGE POINT

(CENTERS FOR DISEASE CONTROL AND THE US GOVERNMENT ACCOUNTABILITY OFFICE EVALUATION REPORT 1987)

Youth who drink alcohol are more likely than their peers to experience:

- school problems, such as higher absence and poor or failing grades;
- social problems, such as fighting and lack of participation in youth activities;
- legal problems, such as arrest for driving or physically hurting someone while drunk;
- physical problems, such as hangovers or illnesses;
- unwanted, unplanned, and unprotected sexual activity;
- disruption of normal growth and sexual development;
- physical and sexual assault;
- higher risk for suicide and homicide;
- alcohol-related car crashes and other unintentional injuries, such as burns, falls, and drowning;
- memory problems;
- abuse of other drugs;
- changes in brain development that may have lifelong effects; and
- death from alcohol poisoning.

In the course of investigating Brian, I determined that he had a period of thirty days when he was neither working nor in school. His employer confirmed that he was not working at his job during the school year, but he was also not in school. In fact, no explanation at all was given for what he was doing during those thirty days. Surely his teachers would have noticed, and the school administration would have had something to say about his absence. Strangely, they refused to comment, even though they knew I was conducting an official government background check for the US Army. Something was up.

I went back to interview Brian's mother (I had already interviewed her during this investigation) to see whether she had any more to say about those mysterious thirty days. When a group of people are attempting to cover something up, they usually have the big pieces of their stories coordinated; therefore it is often the littlest inconsistencies that eventually reveal the truth. Brian's mother let slip that Brian had been working to pay off an engagement ring. Here was something new, an undisclosed debt. I pointed out that Brian had a regular job and his employer had confirmed he had not been working. His mother now said that he had been working for a relative with medical problems. I continued to ask questions, and what I discovered was the following. Brian had been given more than three thousand dollars in credit to buy an engagement ring he couldn't afford for his girlfriend. At the same time, he had a drug problem and spent thirty days in a rehab program. He wasn't able to work a regular job or attend school during those thirty days, but he was allowed to work for a relative from home to attempt to pay off some of his debt. Furthermore, his mother and several of his friends had pooled money to pay for the expensive rehab program.

Brian, in a follow-up interview, confirmed that he had a drug problem he didn't disclose. He confirmed he had made some bad financial decisions and had a big debt he didn't disclose. He also confirmed he had provided false and misleading information on an official government document when applying for the Army. Also, Brian's teachers and family had attempted to cover up for him. Needless to say, he didn't pass the background check. I am not judging Brian or his teachers and family. They probably thought they were doing the right thing by not speaking about Brian's time in rehab. Certainly, it is admirable to help a friend or family member in need by putting them in a drug rehab program and paying for it. The issue with respect to the Army application and background check is that nobody told the truth. It is possible to provide reasonable explanations for your past. Nobody is perfect, but not being honest in a background check, and then lying to cover it up, simply makes any potential problem worse.

Marijuana drug laws in each state are changing all the time. Federal laws for use and possession have *not* changed. It's still a crime. Other drugs, "harder" drugs (like cocaine, heroin, or crystal meth), are illegal in all states. Also, it is illegal to use prescription drugs not written to you by a licensed physician. While some organizations may excuse "experimenting" with marijuana one or two times, any use more than that is no longer "experimentation." Additionally, the use of hard drugs, even one time, *will* preclude you from *ever* being considered for some positions with the federal government. *Onetime experimentation* of anything harder than marijuana will preclude you from ever working in certain law enforcement positions and from working for certain federal agencies.

Now, I know some of you are thinking, "I don't use drugs." Well, what about your friends? If you are with someone who is using or selling illegal drugs and are caught by the police, you can be arrested and charged with possession. Yes, even if you aren't using or carrying. Another true story involves a young man who had graduated from high school, enlisted in the US Army, and was waiting for his report date. One night, he went to visit his cousin. They were hanging out in the local park, sitting at the picnic tables and talking, when his cousin pulled out a marijuana pipe and started smoking it. Someone saw them sitting in the park and called the police. When the two young men saw the police approaching, the cousin put out the pipe and threw it away from them on the ground, but the police saw him. Both the young man and his cousin were arrested for possession of illegal drug paraphernalia. Even though the young man had already enlisted in the US Army, his enlistment was canceled due to this arrest.

If you are a passenger in a car where someone has drugs or drug paraphernalia and the police stop that car, all passengers can be charged with possession. To make matters worse, if the car you are riding in crosses a state line, you can be charged with interstate transport of drugs and drug paraphernalia in addition to the possession charge. Records of these arrests, charges, and convictions never go away. Watch out for the company that you keep.

There is another story of a college football star, whom I'll call Reggie, and his best friend, whom I'll call Benjamin. Reggie was great at football but an average student academically. Reggie had been accepted to college on a full, four-year football scholarship. Needless to say, this was worth a lot. Reggie completed documents for the scholarship on which he indicated he had never been arrested. His statement was false at the time he made it, and I'll return to that in a moment, but the university accepted his documents without further follow-up, trusting that Reggie was telling the truth. This is the case with many applications. They will not conduct a background check but will trust that the information you provide is accurate. That doesn't make it safer to lie on an application. If the truth comes out and it is different from what you said it was, it's just as big a deal.

Reggie had lied on his application. While he had been in high school, he had been dating a girl two years younger than he, and the two of them had been sexually active. This, by itself, wasn't the problem, but he had passed his eighteenth birthday, and she was not yet eighteen, which, unfortunately for Reggie, made him guilty of statutory rape. Furthermore, the girl's father did not approve of the relationship. When the father discovered that his daughter and Reggie were sexually active (and I don't know how he found out, but it isn't the point), he confronted Reggie and told him to leave his daughter alone. Reggie became angry and violent and physically assaulted the father. The police were called, and Reggie was arrested. Reggie's parents, his illicit girlfriend, her parents, and Reggie's best friend, Benjamin, were all aware of what had happened. Reggie's parents, to keep this story quiet, made some arrangement (I don't know what but probably financial) with the girlfriend's father to keep him from pressing charges. Therefore, Reggie was released without further incident. Still, this was a permanent part of Reggie's past. When presented with a full scholarship to a good college and the potential future of a professional football career, Reggie chose to keep this a secret.

Reggie and Benjamin had known each other since childhood, and as best friends from childhood do, they assumed they would always be friends and made some plans accordingly. Reggie had promised Benjamin that when Reggie became a professional football player, Benjamin would be his manager. The truth is friends from childhood, and even from high school, don't always stay friends through college and after. People change a lot as they age from child to adolescent to adult. Also, as you go from grade school to high school to college, you meet many more people. As Reggie went from high school to college and became more and more involved in his college football program, he spoke less and less to Benjamin. It became clear to Benjamin that he was being left behind, and he decided to take revenge. He revealed to the football coach, the dean of students, the university president, and the local newspaper that Reggie had a past arrest for assault and sexual involvement with a minor. The university could not ignore this. Reggie was expelled. You might think that Benjamin ruined his friend's academic and football career, or you might think that Benjamin was just getting the truth out in the open. Regardless, Reggie paid the price for not disclosing his past arrest at the time it would have done the least damage (on the scholarship form) and for trusting a friend who wasn't worthy. Be careful what information you share with your friends, but also, be sure on a background check to be complete and truthful. It is not necessarily the case that one past incident will derail your entire future.

KNOWLEDGE POINT

Statutory rape is a generic term describing no forced sexual activity where one of the individuals is below the age of consent. It can be particularly problematic for high school students who begin dating before either has legally become an adult, and then one turns eighteen before the other, and they are sexually active. Only a few states have special laws to treat this all-too-common event. In most states, the legal adult can now be prosecuted for rape even though the ages separating the individuals may only be a few months.

Bullying can have terrible consequences for both the person being bullied and the bully. I'm sure you've seen stories in the news about people killing themselves because of bullying. Bullying can happen in person, but it can also happen online. Online bullying even has a name: cyberbullying. Bullying is a crime, and people have been convicted of crimes related to incidents of bullying. If you think it's just fun to pick on someone at school, think again.

There was a fourteen-year-old middle-school student, Calvin, who was regularly bullied for being a little "slow." The only person who would talk to him was another fourteen-year-old student, Ross. Ross found out that a woman who was a neighbor of Calvin was a drug dealer. Ross talked Calvin into helping him break into the woman's apartment when they thought she was not there in order to steal money. As a kid who was bullied, it was perhaps hard for Calvin to say no to the only person who would talk to him. As it turned out, the neighbor was home, and Ross raped and killed her. Even though Calvin did not kill her, he broke into the apartment. Although he was fourteen years old, he was tried as an adult, found guilty of second-degree murder, and sentenced to twenty-five years in jail.

If I sound like a parent in this chapter, remember, I am one. I am also an investigator with decades of experience uncovering other people's histories. I am amazed at some of the stupid or awful things people have done. Some people are beyond hope. No matter what, they are going to get into trouble. For most of the rest, a little bit of clear thinking and better judgment would have served them well and helped them avoid a problem that will now be a permanent part of their past. This chapter is directed at those people. Think before you act. Try to imagine what could go wrong and how bad the consequences could be if something does go wrong. Your future is counting on it!

Overcoming and surviving the challenges young adults face in today's world.
youak/DigitalVision Vectors via Getty Images

QUESTIONS TO CONSIDER

1. What are some of my concerns about my life challenges?
2. Do I have secrets from my past history that could cause problems in my future plans?
3. How does Evon's story relate to the events in my life?

4. How do the information and facts provided help me to prepare for the investigative inquiry/background check questionnaire?
5. What am I doing to make necessary changes in my life to address potential problems in the investigative process?
6. How is my relationship with my friends and their lifestyles impacting my life with regard to understanding and following the guidelines, laws, and rules of society?

5

Moving On from Your Past

Up until now, I have been telling you what you should and should not do, but what if you have already done some of what you should not do? What if there are some things in your past that you are not proud of? Is all lost? No. I am going to talk about what you can do to navigate through the challenges that may already be a part of your life and that will be a part of a future background investigation of you.

I grew up in a small town in Mississippi in the 1960s and 1970s, and parenting was a community activity. It was not just my parents who watched over me but other family members, my neighbors, my friends' parents, the teachers at my school, and even church elders. All of my friends, in fact, every kid in town, were in the same boat. Whatever we did, we were always under the watchful eyes of the adults in town. I am not saying this was good or bad. It was just a fact of small-town life in rural Mississippi at that time. We did not have much interaction with the rest of the world if it existed more than twenty-five miles from home. During this period of my life, my biggest concerns and challenges were getting into a fight with another boy, going someplace I had been told not to go, or hanging out with the "wrong" kids or adults. The punishment for any of these actions would be a "talking-to" and a reminder not to do it again. I quickly learned that I did not have much to be concerned about.

Following my family's move in the 1970s from Mississippi to Illinois, the challenges became far more of a real concern with life-and-death results on the line. Fortunately for me, the positive impact of my community upbringing in Mississippi helped me to get through the new world in which I was living in Illinois. It was here I went to junior high and high school. I saw neighbors involved in domestic situations, alcoholic abuse, and illegal drug use. At school, I saw students involved in drugs and alcohol. I saw violent attacks by some of the older kids against students and some teachers. As any kid would have been, I was tempted to get involved with illegal drugs and use alcohol with some of the guys when I was invited to parties, but somehow, I did not. Somehow, perhaps because of the strong adult role models from my youth in Mississippi, I was able to avoid getting into any real trouble. I never wanted to get into trouble because I felt I could have fun without getting all "crazy" or trying to be like somebody else. Because of my upbringing, I felt that doing the "right thing" was also the "right thing" for me personally, so I never felt conflicted.

That was not true for a good friend of mine, who grew up with more challenges and, as he stated, more temptation and interest to explore the opportunities of his youth. My friend got into trouble often. He got into a bad situation when he was growing up that resulted in school suspensions and later an arrest, for which he received probation from the court. In addition, his use of illegal drugs and getting caught with the wrong crowd as a teenager consuming alcohol while riding in a speeding car also created a criminal record. Why did he do this? My friend told me that he felt that he had to be a part of a "cool" group to have friends and to be a part of what he thought was the social scene of the time. Clearly, he was not alone. There were many kids just like him, and that is true in every generation. Junior high, high school, and college are when you move beyond the influence of your parents and start making your own decisions and acting independently. Of course, you have to live with the decisions you make, but just because you make some bad choices does not mean your future is ruined. My friend made some bad choices and had to live with them, but he also did some good things. For one thing, he accepted the consequences. My friend learned from his actions and decided that he did not want to give up on his future, even though he had an arrest record. He completed high school, went to college, and fulfilled his dream of becoming a successful professional. He is a high-ranking government official because he owned his past but did not let it define him.

What did he do to overcome his criminal record? Every time he applied for school or for a job, he admitted to his past. He never tried to hide it. Also, he explained that he knew the actions that led to his arrest were wrong and he had learned from them. He also demonstrated that he was not a repeat offender. When you are young and your arrest is in the very recent past, of course, you cannot prove that "it hasn't happened again." The longer you go without an event on your criminal record, however, the more it supports the claim that you learned your lesson. It is possible to overcome a criminal history. The key to moving forward through life (so that you do not have to worry about a background investigation) is not to continue or repeat the "bad things" that led to an arrest, illegal drug possession, alcohol abuse, or credit account problems.

KNOWLEDGE POINT

The background investigation process does not penalize you for your past actions. Admitting to something in your past will not lead to further punishment.

I do not want to give the impression that I was always a perfect child. When I went away to college, I experimented with drugs and alcohol, as most kids who go to college do, though it is not something I condone. College is often a liberating time for young people. The most common experience for college students is to live away from the home where they grew up, in student housing or a rental apartment. Therefore, it is the first time that they are living entirely free of their parents' supervision. Imagine not being told when to go to bed or when to get up, when or what to eat, when to do your homework or when to be home. You are expected to figure those things out on your own. You will have classes and homework, but the college will not force you to attend. There will simply be consequences if you do not (like expulsion). Nevertheless, you get to make your own choices. Within that freedom are the opportunities to experiment with alcohol, drugs, your sexuality, and many other things. As is often the case with trying new things, many young people do the things they like, such as drinking or drugs, to excess. It is only natural. To find your comfort zone, you often have to experience the unpleasantness of exceeding your limits. The problem with drinking too much or doing drugs is that your judgment becomes impaired and your inhibitions lowered. For drinking, the act itself is illegal if you are underage. For most drugs, it does not matter what age you are: they are illegal. Furthermore, when you do careless, dangerous, or foolish things, if those actions are also illegal, the problems multiply.

Your past may already include an official record of an unfortunate incident with alcohol or drugs. After all, almost everyone, at some point or other, drinks too much, and many people try drugs. If you are worried about this being disclosed in a background investigation, remember that the investigation is not looking at your history to punish you further. It is looking to determine whether you have a problem. If you are honest about a problem and can demonstrate that you have paid the appropriate dues to society and that you have learned not to repeat the illegal behavior, you can very likely get past the problem in the investigation.

Some events in your past may have been due to your own irresponsibility, while others may have been due to your age, family, social network, or simply a lack of understanding of the consequences of your actions. Through your honesty, you let people know that you have learned from your past and have moved on. You should never attempt to hide the negative events in your past. Remember that we live in the age of information. The truth is it is almost impossible to conceal your past from a trained, professional investigator if they have sufficient time. As William Shakespeare wrote, "The truth will out." If you attempt to lie or conceal in a thorough background investigation, small inconsistencies will likely lead the investigator to discover the lie. Now you have doubled your problems.

If you are curious to know what an investigator is likely to discover about you in even a simple investigation, perform your own investigation on yourself. Google yourself. Examine all of your social media accounts from the point of view of someone who does not know you. Ask yourself, honestly, what you would think of what you discovered if "you" were someone you did not know. Also, be prepared to dispute any information you discover about yourself that is factually wrong. You should know what can be found about yourself, but you do not have to let incorrect or misleading information about you remain unchallenged.

Also, select someone who knows you well and has known you a while, such as a family friend, to serve as a character reference. It must be someone you trust because you must be willing to tell them everything about your past, good and bad, so that they can address those events in letters or interviews during your background check. I cannot stress enough the need for the reference to be knowledgeable of your past and aware that you are listing them as a reference regarding the background check or investigation. A good personal reference can vouch for your character and present the case for why you are a good and deserving person. Provide references that will be able to speak truthfully and positively about you.

It is part of human nature that we all make mistakes in life, but those mistakes do not have to define you. How you meet and respond to those mistakes is also a testament to the kind of person you are. A background investigation is designed to compile the facts of your past and present them in a clear report. Ultimately, it will be another person, not an unfeeling machine, who evaluates you based on that report. That person is themselves human, has made their own mistakes, and may have been given the benefit of the doubt despite their past to get where they are now. Rely on them to do the same for you during your background check, provided you are candid and honest about your history. It is possible to overcome unfortunate circumstance in your past. Reveal; do not conceal.

SUNNY'S STORY

One of the most interesting success stories I have encountered as an investigator had many challenges that a lot of young adults may not have survived like Sunny did (names and other related personal information have been changed in this story). Sunny was born in the rural area of southern Mississippi and lived there until she was ten years old. At that time, she and her mother moved to New Orleans. They lived in the projects in the Ninth Ward of New Orleans, where she witnessed many violent and disturbing acts and events. Sunny was the child of a single mother with alcohol problems and an unknown father who had enlisted in the military and never recontacted her mother or her. Sunny's life developed around her interest in reading books at the library and watching educational programs on TV. Her transition from her school in Mississippi to the Catholic school in New Orleans her mother had been able to get her in allowed her to make significant progress in her education—from a fifth-grade level to a ninth-grade level of understanding and achievement. Sunny's increased level of achievement caught the attention of one of her teachers and an advisor. Both the teacher and the counselor decided that they would do everything they could to see that Sunny had the opportunity and access to all the books, documents, and contacts with colleges and institutions that would be interested in a student with her learning level and current achievement. Through her teacher and counselor, Sunny was able to move beyond her classmates at her school and reach the education level of a twelfth grader in the tenth grade.

At home, Sunny's life was very unstable. Her mother continued to abuse alcohol and brought different men in and out of her life. Sunny would tell years later of two incidents where she was sexually abused and raped by one man and had also been involved with a man (as his girlfriend) who her mother was also seeing, to the point that she believed he would take her away from the life she was living. Throughout all this activity at home and in the neighborhood, Sunny had steered clear of alcohol and drugs, as well as the criminal activities of some of her mother's friends.

Sunny had begun to realize that school and the opportunities that it offered were the best way—and her only way—out of the projects. After taking several exams and evaluations, Sunny was given the opportunity to graduate early from high school and was also provided several scholarship offers and grants to attend college. Through the guidance and assistance of her teacher and counselor, Sunny chose to go to Georgetown University in Washington, D.C., with a full scholarship. In addition to this selection, Sunny had expressed her interest in studying abroad when the opportunity presented itself.

Sunny graduated from high school and started college in Washington, D.C., where she would be on her own with limited support and no family members around. Sunny's start in college went well—she was successful in all her classes and made friends with her new roommate in the dorm. After two years in college, the opportunity of studying abroad presented itself. After completing the application process and receiving approval from the department chairman and financial support based on her grades and achievements, Sunny was on her way to France. Prior to leaving for France, Sunny and all those traveling from the university were briefed by Department of State officials regarding security procedures and protocols and specifics regarding foreign contacts and events. The importance of this briefing would come back to haunt Sunny in her future opportunities during her application process with the US government.

When Sunny arrived in Paris, France, she was accompanied by a department advisor, two fellow classmates, and a point of contact from the French university partnership group. The program established at that time provided for the visiting student to participate in university classes and designated assignments and activities on and off campus. Sunny stated that during an after-hours event at a pub, she met another student who said he was from Germany. She had two drinks with this student (prior to this event, Sunny had only had a small number of alcoholic beverages in college) and returned to the hotel where she was staying without incident. Sunny did not report this after-hours foreign contact and event to her advisor. It is important at this time to remember Sunny's past interactions with the male figures in her life and to know that she had kept her past a secret from her advisor and classmates.

Over the next several weeks, Sunny did well with her classes and assignments and continued to meet and spend time with her German friend (Boris) at different places around the city. During these social events, Sunny started to drink more alcoholic beverages and experiment with illegal substances (such as marijuana). During this study abroad program, Sunny had been advised that there was limited interaction with the US Department of State's embassy staff and more contact with individuals from the various educational institutions of students studying there from around the world (Germany, England, Turkey, Russia, Egypt, and Israel, among a few other countries represented there). Sunny had by this time started a relationship with Boris, and her use of alcohol and illegal substances was getting out of control. At one point, Sunny used a small amount of cocaine to get high with Boris, and her activities caught the attention of both her classmates and the advisor. Sunny was brought into the office for an evaluation and was questioned on the recent changes in her life. Sunny admitted to having contact with a foreign national and to her use and abuse of alcohol and illegal substances. She also admitted to not being truthful about her conduct, as required while a student in the study abroad program.

Because of her university and study abroad program student violations, Sunny's case was presented to the dean of the department. The dean determined that Sunny's actions and decisions were serious violations and demanded she be immediately dismissed. Sunny was also found to be academically ineligible for financial support for any type of educational opportunities and was dismissed from the university for a transfer to another college or university. Unfortunately, because of this action by the university, Sunny was forced to leave the university and the city before she could receive any real help for her personal problems with alcohol and drugs, which she now found herself addicted to. Sunny, with the assistance of her former roommate and high school advisor in New Orleans, was able to return to New Orleans to live with her advisor.

Following the actions that occurred in France and the decision of the university, Sunny found herself back where she started from. Sunny had told her former advisor, Mrs. Allen, all about her success at Georgetown and her selection to the study abroad program that paid for her travel to Paris, France, where she met the young man who said that he was from Germany and the relationship that developed between them over a short period of weeks. Sunny then told her something that she had not told anyone else while in France or back at the university in Washington, D.C.: she had been raped by this young man (Boris) and had contracted a sexually transmitted disease.

Mrs. Allen took Sunny into her home and, along with her spouse, helped Sunny get into a drug rehabilitation program and a community college to continue her education. Sunny began to understand the meaning of family, support, living, and learning. Over the next two years, through the assistance and contacts of Mrs. Allen, Sunny was able to complete courses at the community college and was accepted into the

University of Texas college system in the Dallas–Fort Worth metro area with financial assistance.

When Sunny restarted her educational journey at the University of Texas, she looked at outside opportunities that would offer her an internship either in one of the government departments or in the courts in the Dallas–Fort Worth area and eventually back in Washington, D.C., at the federal level. Sunny continued to focus on any opportunity that would provide for an internship with a government agency while attending classes and placing herself in the spotlight through her academic achievements. It was during her second year at University of Texas that she received information through her departmental contacts that an internship position was available with one of the state court judges in the Dallas area and that she should apply for consideration for this position. Sunny had been noticed by a member of the judicial board who was a professor at the university and would be the one who conducted her interview and made the recommendation for her to serve as a part-time intern with the judge at the state court–level division in Dallas for six months. Sunny started the intern project with the judge and continued her education at the university full-time and managed to be successful doing both.

Following her acceptance into the university in Dallas, she had continued to keep herself out of trouble by not drinking any alcoholic beverages and not using any illegal substances. Sunny had also made a decision to attend Alcoholic Anonymous (AA) on a regular basis to keep herself on track. This commitment to move forward through AA, classes, an internship, and positive people had made the difference in her quality of life.

Following her third year at the university and after completing her six-month internship with an "outstanding" rating from the judge, Sunny received a call with the invitation she had dreamed about: the opportunity to serve an internship in the federal government. It was at this point I first made contact with Sunny and would learn of her story through the background investigation process and through a mentoring program I was a part of for two years. My contact with Sunny would become one of the best stories of overcoming childhood poverty, family dysfunction, sexual abuse, rape, drug use, alcohol abuse, and being expelled/dismissed from one of the top ten educational institutions in the United States for her personal conduct and activities while on a study abroad program in France. Through the many investigations I have conducted throughout my time with the government and with corporate cases, Sunny's life story has all the reasons to give up and step away from the possibility of having any chance of success in your lifelong dreams and goals. When I first received Sunny's documentation and read the many pages of activities and events she had listed in her background, I was shocked and amazed of the past-to-present steps she had made from high school attendance in New Orleans, college attendance in Washington, D.C., and her return to New Orleans and the decisions she made to overcome her past and "get it right" for her future.

My first in-person contact with Sunny was positive and refreshing. Through the initial background investigations candidate interview, there is the review of the entire SF-86 or other official documents used to gather the history of an individual from their eighteenth birthday forward. Sunny was open and up-front and provided full disclosure about her past. She stated that she had no problem in talking about the various events that occurred in her life. Sunny's selection for the internship program required that she also undergo additional investigative responses to specific questions by the department and even a polygraph exam if necessary. Sunny provided a written statement where required of her use of illegal substances, her abuse of alcohol, and her contact with the foreign national and failure to disclose their relationship. Sunny outlined her story, provided Mrs. Allen as a reference, and willingly talked about every detail that led her to become the person she was that day. Sunny understood the importance of being honest and truthful about her past actions and activities no matter how bad or disturbing they might have been.

The candidate/personal interview is an opportunity to provide the "road map" of your life, past to present, with all the distractions, unexpected events, side stops, and changes that were necessary to get to your destination. Following Sunny's completion of the interview and the other investigative requirements, she was selected and placed in the government agency that was interested in her. Sunny completed her summer internship and was asked to come back after her senior year and work full time in the agency's legal department with options to attend college for a higher degree with financial support. Sunny was successful in completing her senior year in college and graduating with a 3.90 on a 4.0 scale. She also received university honors for additional academic achievement and community service with young adults.

Sunny's achievements and success in college and her entry into the government demonstrate an incredible story of overcoming a mountain of challenges and problems in life. Sunny went on to become a successful administrator in the government and worked in the private sector, where she received several promotions and assignments across the country and made a few trips overseas as well. Sunny would also return home to provide assistance, directions, and financial support to the mentoring programs in Dallas and in New Orleans.

The objective of sharing this story is to let you know that no matter what has happened to you, what is happening to you, or what may happen to you, you can get through it with strength, desire, willpower, and a strong support system (family, friends, and faith). You must not be afraid to reach out to others, especially those that you have learned to trust and depend on in your life. And through all the things that happen in your life, as you move forward, you have to remember that the past is your history and you cannot go back and change any of it. What you can do is to learn from your past and make better decisions with your choices of friends, activities, and events you involve yourself in. You then have to be up-front and open when seeking employment opportunities, going into the military, or other important phases in your life. Always provide the truth and tell the story about who you were and who you have become.

MARLA'S STORY

I met Marla (name and background information have been changed) when conducting a background investigation on her when she applied for a position requiring a complete ten-year background investigation for a secret-level government job. During the interview process, it came out that she has suffered from bipolar affective disorder type II since the age of sixteen. Marla suffers from a complex, long-term condition that brings with it periods of depression, hypomania, mania, and stability.

While the law (federal and most states) forbids a company from hiring or firing based on this medical condition, Marla has found through the years that such discrimination still occurs. It has made her hesitant to share her disorder when applying for jobs. But she hopes that one day the stigma surrounding mental health will ease and people can be open and honest without the fear of it affecting their position. This is her story:

> Years after my initial diagnosis, much has changed in my life and yet much has not in terms of the stigma and discrimination I have experienced, due to my condition. My experience of the disorder is as different to that of someone else as two fish swimming in the same ocean with distinctly different colors of their scales. Bipolar is my best friend and my worst enemy; it can be refreshing and bring with it a range of creativity but also be destructive and hard to rebuild from in the wake of its damage. There are many assumptions that people make about bipolar disorder that are false. The number one assumption I have encountered is that bipolar is just mood swings and either being happy or sad, yet it is so much more than that. Hearing people jokingly say, "I'm so bipolar!" sets my teeth on edge. It is in fact a complex, long-term condition with sufferers all having different periods of depression, hypomania, mania, and stability. Mania for me is reckless, dangerous driving. It is spending masses of money I do not have. It is an irrational, intense anger toward

everything and everyone. It is believing I can rule the world and anything is possible. Paranoia follows me everywhere, whispering in my ear. It is hearing voices that boost my self-belief.

This all very suddenly turns into depression, and I am left feeling physically and emotionally exhausted. I begin to fixate and obsess on all the outlandish and embarrassing things I did when I was manic and hate myself for it. The depression will become so severe I will become suicidal and make plans to end my life. Bipolar mania and depression can sometimes be accompanied by psychosis. When I am very depressed, I will hear voices that are malicious and hurtful. Many people with bipolar, including myself, also suffer from anxiety, problems with addiction, and eating disorders.

There is a secret, one that nobody is prepared to talk about, one so shocking it may bring down society as we know it. Am I talking about a scandal or some sort of political corruption? Am I talking about some secret society that quietly rules over us, or perhaps I am talking about the fact we are all lizard people? While I would infinitely prefer to talk about any one of these things, I am in fact talking about the truth that, literally, nobody is talking about. I am talking about the fact that people with mental illness walk among us.

I hear your gasps and sighs; "not this again," "haven't we already talked about this?" and trust me, I hear you. In essence you are right; people with mental illness are no longer labeled as "crazy" or "psychos" and that is great, it really is, but the sad truth is we're not being talked about as real people either. We are not seen as human beings who happen to have various conditions, but we are in fact seen as the embodiment of the conditions themselves. I suffer with bipolar and yet many people feel obliged to tell me that I "am" bipolar. How would you feel if I said that you "were" varicose veins or you "were" diabetes?

The fact is that people with mental illness are not often talked about badly anymore; it seems we are just, quite simply, not talked about, not in any meaningful way anyway. I see people putting up posts on my Facebook all the time, with one-off little comments on how they have struggled, and that is great—more power to them—but these are just fleeting moments of support that quickly fizzle and burn out. There is no substance to them.

In the time since I was diagnosed, I have worked abroad in several different countries and experienced both direct and firsthand intolerance and misunderstanding. I have experienced the struggle of living with the condition at work, at home, in my relationships, and with my family. It has lost me jobs, damaged my friendships, challenged my romantic relationships, and affected the well-being of my family.

People assume that if you have bipolar disorder, you're going to be challenging at work or difficult to be around. This causes many sufferers to feel isolated and alone. It's caused me to answer "I'm fine" when I've felt desolate inside so as not to cause a fuss. I used to worry about people finding out and thinking I was mad or fear that they may never understand. I have not disclosed at interview[s] or when I've started a job, out of worry that they would find some other excuse not to employ me. I have lied to past employers about why I've been off sick. It shouldn't be this way and often makes a difficult episode of depression or mania even more severe because of the stress all the stigma creates.

Even today in the United States, it is easier to say, "I have constant back pain" than "I have bipolar," as it can risk you losing a job, not being hired, being misunderstood, and being made to be a social pariah. I am one of the lucky ones, living in a society where the law and charities such as Mind and Time to Change work to end the problems people with the condition face.

I do not regret the condition—only the damage it has done to my nearest and dearest. Ultimately it is my cross to bear. I wait for a day when a person with bipolar is looked at, judged, and supported in the same way as someone with a physical ailment, when the brain and mind are treated as if they were any part of the human body.

Some people with mental illness are proactive in getting the word out there, but many are afraid to, out of fear and stigma. Maybe if we talked more, we would find that people are more tolerant than we think. This is not supposed to be a rant at people; it is merely supposed to be a message that what we say is important and can make a huge difference.

People with mental illness are not locked away, nor are they off in the distance somewhere; they are here with us. They are our doctors, our friends, our mothers, our firefighters. They are our partners, our siblings, our teachers, and they are allowed to have bad days. So, next time you are out at the pub or about to make a Facebook post, next time you go shopping with your friend or you stop for a five-minute chat in your lunch break, just remember this piece and maybe try to talk about it. You never know, you might just be surprised.

The background investigative process now provides in some cases for medical professionals to assist someone like Marla who is going through the counseling and treatment programs to seek professional employment opportunities. A limited question-and-answer process asks: (1) What is the diagnosis? (2) What is the period and treatment plan provided? (3) What is the prognosis going forward? These questions provide a look into a person's past and current situation, which will provide critical answers when evaluating one's eligibility for employment with the government. In the 1970s, 1980s, and 1990s, there was a more extensive list of medical-related treatment and program questions that resulted in many individuals not applying for certain jobs and most medical professionals refusing to respond to the many questions about their patient's past and present circumstances. Now, you have the opportunity to be considered and may (in some cases) even be able to continue your treatment into your new employment. This can be said for both the corporate and government sectors today, and through new medical programs and the use of social media, there are more resources and acceptance in the world.

QUESTIONS TO CONSIDER
1. Am I ready to respond with the truth about my history in a background investigation?
2. Can I disclose the worst event(s) that happened in my life to others?
3. Are there activities and events in my past that I have yet to change that if known would cause concerns and issues in my future employment opportunities?

4. Who are the people (references and verifiers) that know about my true past?
5. If not now, when will I make the necessary changes in my life to live in the present and not the past?
6. Where am I with my career interests and goals for my future?
7. Who am I, then and now?
8. How am I doing in my life?

Methods, techniques, and personal options through your challenges. *Enis Aksoy/DigitalVision Vectors via Getty Images*

6

Undergoing a Background Check for Your Security Clearance

In this chapter, I will explain why investigations are important in our society and in the daily operations of many of our corporations, businesses, and governments (state and federal). There are several types of investigations that I will discuss with you in this chapter in order to provide you with a better understanding of this topic. There are background checks, background investigations, and what I call security checks. The general purpose of these investigations is to conduct research, gather information, and identify relevant issues, facts, and concerns regarding individual candidates for consideration of employment.

The basic difference between investigations from businesses, corporations, and governments is the research conducted by human resource departments of the private-sector investigations and the more in-depth review regarding past and current events in the candidate's overall history. In addition to the federal government, various state governments and law enforcement agencies are part of the more in-depth review.

Let us look at some of the types of investigations that are used the most as part of a candidate's hiring review process.

BACKGROUND CHECK

First there is the background check. The background check is completed through the human resources and/or security departments of the individual companies and businesses. HumanResources.com reported that over 96 percent of employers conduct at least one type of background check. The objective for these companies is to confirm that potential candidates are exactly who they say they are and that their listed information—education, work history, and noncriminal records—are verifiable. The focus or key objectives are to review a candidate's education, credit history, driving record, criminal record, work history, and use of social media. Also, some companies and businesses conduct drug screenings and review medical history. Additionally, there are now more paid services (Internet-based data-gathering companies) that can provide employers with a wealth of public information organized in a single prepared report, such as the Internet-based companies Been-Verified, Truth Finder, and Check Mate. These new types of services encourage candidates to be more forthcoming about their background history. These reports will include employment history, financial records (credit reports), criminal records, and court records. This type of report is a snapshot of the candidate's past life and current status; in other words, it will include some of the things you did in your teen years and what has changed now that you are over eighteen and in the next phase of your young adult life. The following are how investigative reports are useful in the background check process:

1. Criminal Background Checks—these checks are for minor and major criminal activity, such as arrests, embezzlement, felony convictions, fraud, and/or violent or sexual crimes.
2. E-Verify Checks—these checks verify the candidate's identity and employment eligibility.
3. Fingerprint Checks—these checks are mandatory for government (state and federal) candidates and provide information on a person's criminal history from authorized criminal justice agencies.
4. Federal Government—Office of the Inspector General—this check reviews health care–related criminal history regarding candidates applying for government jobs and/or government contracts.

5. Credit Checks—these types of checks are used for most candidates and especially for those applying for financial positions, such as banks and credit-related organizations and businesses. A close review will be done regarding payment history, including unpaid accounts in collections, bankruptcies, tax liens, judgments, and recent credit inquiries on the candidate.
6. Driver's License—this check verifies the candidate's valid state-issued driver's license.
7. International Checks—for those who have had internships or study abroad programs through colleges and universities in other countries, investigations will be conducted directly with the institution and/or company in that country. In Europe, for example, the check might be done through "Interpol" (the International Criminal Police Organization), which is the international organization that facilitates worldwide police cooperation and crime control and is based in Lyon, France. This international law enforcement agency assists United States agencies (the FBI and state agencies like the Florida Department of Law Enforcement [FDLE]) and other reporting (private) companies that pay a fee for information with verification of a candidate's residence, employment, education, and international criminal records, and, in specific cases, contacts for the reported internships and study abroad programs and employment in the listed countries.

Let us take a closer look at how and why this process is important, starting with the employment investigations. Based on my research, I would venture to say that seven out of ten employers investigate the background of potential employees by looking at specific areas such as credit, criminal history, and reference checks at a minimum. For employers, performing a background check is their opportunity to verify information provided by the job applicant. The results may reveal information that was either mistakenly or intentionally omitted, such as an arrest in another state where the applicant lived at one time, and verification of the applicant's certifications and degrees. Colleges, universities, health care/medical institutions, and some banks, for example, will disclose that applicants who are being considered for high-risk positions may be liable for negligent hiring or retention if this employee is later involved in harmful misconduct or illegal activities. The cost for these businesses and institutions would be expensive. Many corporate boards and legal departments as well as risk management personnel require this process to be completed on new applicants in order to promote a safe workplace, and it is a tool that has proven to reduce the odds of bad hires. The following were provided by several companies as major reasons for conducting background checks on all job applicants:

1. encourage honesty in the application and interview process;
2. discourage candidates with possible issues and activities to hide;
3. eliminate uncertainty in the employment hiring process;
4. hire the best qualified people that will contribute to the growth of the business and not bring "baggage" with them;
5. provide a safe and secure workplace environment for employees and clients;
6. minimize exposure from employee liability by practicing the "due diligence" process with all new hires;
7. protect the company from negligent hiring;
8. provide a direct message to candidates and the public about the company's objectives and methods in the workforce environment;
9. confirm the company's drug-free workplace environment for all; and
10. verify the candidate's claims, qualifications, and listed credentials.

With the rise of information technology systems and the Internet in general, companies have discovered more inaccuracies and discrepancies about potential candidates for employment. The background check is an essential part of the verification of claims made by the candidate during the course of the application process and before a final decision is made by the company on the candidate. I am sure some of you are aware through social media and TV that candidates for various positions (sometimes entry level and other times management and above) have provided fake resumes, degrees, and a list of faked references. The background check provides a level of verification that the candidate's education, credentials, and job history are "what they say they are." The background check provides the objective data to help companies and businesses determine if a potential candidate is appropriate for the position and work environment based on their experience, education, and training. In other words, you now have a view of the candidate beyond what is included on their resume or through an interview.

Hiring highly qualified candidates is essential to every company's success. The background screening and investigations process is a crucial guide to success in a challenging business environment. One of those crucial components of the hiring process has become (and should be) the employment background screening, pre- and post-hire, which provides hiring personnel a view into the candidate's past behavior patterns, propensities, and "likely" future behavior. Knowing that this background process exists will encourage future applicants to be more forthcoming about their past activities and actions. A quote I heard years ago regarding the view of one's past actions and behaviors is "You can't be a twenty-seven-year-old acting and doing things as if you are a seventeen-year-old teenager." You have to continue to move forward through the timeline of your life. The background investigation specifically investigates and reviews your life from the age of eighteen onward. In other words, what criminal or unlawful actions, such as use of illegal drugs, abuse of alcoholic beverages, speeding tickets, loud noise, and other violations that are typical and well documented for young adults from the age of fourteen to eighteen years old determined the necessary level of concern, involvement, and overall future issues, which are a part of the age and time period of your life. Other investigations and the background check/security inquiry are designed to look at the information disclosed or in some cases discovered from the most recent events and activities and your immediate past that go against company policies and any agreement or acceptance of the questions for employment.

As you as a young adult prepare your resume for presentation and review by the human resource professionals in the near future, you are on "notice" with information and inside knowledge as to what to expect and prepare for your first job or your first career-related application process.

SECURITY CHECKS

Over the past two years, the security investigative check (an investigation described by many security professionals used for the purpose of researching information on a candidate/applicant that can be "trusted" if selected for employment) process has been highlighted in media reports and security documentaries and has disclosed problems with the screening systems used by some school districts and colleges and universities across the United States. The Chicago public school district recently banned 266 employees from returning to work following a background check that disclosed a history of (1) violence, (2) sexual misconduct, and (3) dangerous criminal activity. The report states that more than one in four were teachers. The *Chicago Tribune* also found that "some of the school district employees who had abused students also have arrest records." When searching through articles regarding safety programs or the background systems currently used, I found that the state of North Carolina does not have a (statewide) policy on the fingerprinting of potential employees or follow-up fingerprinting of current staff and/or teachers. The state of North Carolina allows individual counties to conduct their own background checks to include fingerprinting and/or criminal records checks. After finding out about this process, I have to say that students, parents, and teachers should be alarmed and concerned about what background check/investigation is used in their school district. The objective has to be providing the educational opportunities to students, while protecting students from the people who bring with them a criminal history and other dangerous activities that could endanger the lives of all at our institutions of learning.

As schools, colleges, and universities are experiencing discoveries of missed criminal activities, sexual offenders, and other offenses of current employees, they are having to take major steps to protect all personnel and specifically the students that they are entrusted to care for. Some of those actions include the following policies and procedures:

1. Create a standard background procedure for screening of all personnel.
2. Collect and check potential and current employees' fingerprints (some colleges and universities are checking students who are a part of the athletic departments).
3. Check all local, county, state, and national criminal databases to include the sex-offender database.
4. Require all candidates to provide complete, accurate, and consistent information.
5. Screen all vendors, contractors, volunteers, and temporary employees.
6. Review and verify the credentials, past employment, and education of all candidates.
7. Review motor vehicle reports.
8. Conduct background checks/screenings on a periodic basis of current employees.
9. Conduct drug screening and other related testing of candidates and follow-up of current employees.

These updates and/or changes to the background check/screening process will allow for school, colleges, and universities to (a) identify an individual's arrest record and criminal history, (b) identify candidates who are registered sex offenders, (c) identify a candidate's employment eligibility through verification of sources, and (d) identify any misleading information, like phony college degrees, professional certifications, previous job titles, and areas of responsibilities. One area that is also an issue is financial-related problems when individuals are placed in a position of handling money or overseeing fundraising projects for the students at schools and some colleges. Additionally, the other area discussed on media outlets is vehicle accidents by school bus drivers and other employees using official vehicles while under the influence or reckless driving. The background check is a requirement and a major part of the employment entry and continuing process for a safe and secure environment.

For those of you planning on going to college and playing any type of sports, be prepared to go through a background check/investigation process that will at a minimum check the basic information available through the services stated above.

In 2010, *Sports Illustrated* published a story regarding criminal background checks on college students who were athletes in college and university programs. They reported that "70% of the players in the preseason Top 25, a total of 204 student-athletes, had been charged with or cited for a crime, and dozens of players had multiple arrests on their records." This was a shock at that time and would be even more alarming in today's college and university sports programs across the country.

Sports Illustrated went on to report that "virtually all coaches interviewed had no idea." In addition, only two of the twenty-five colleges in the investigation (Texas Christian University [TCU] and the University of Oklahoma) ran any type of criminal background checks on recruits. During this time period, neither TCU nor Oklahoma conducted any inquiries into the recruits' juvenile record—in fact, not a single college did. At the time of this media investigation by *Sports Illustrated*, the response from colleges and other officials was that "in the future, student-athletes hoping to play at the college level may soon be facing background checks in their recruiting future."

Information gathering and sharing through technology resources. *sesame/ DigitalVision Vectors via Getty Images*

BACKGROUND INVESTIGATIONS

Like businesses and the government agencies responsible for research-ing and collecting information on prospective candidates, schools and colleges must now consider a "deeper" look into students entering into specific programs in order to know the truth about the person work-ing and attending classes as part of the general population of these institutions. Also, as young adults, given the various incidents of the past years of violent acts and attacks on fellow students, this action will provide a sense of awareness and involvement of the safety and security process that is designed to protect you. When I learn about the new and continuing developments for students, I am relieved and happy to know that the concerns and problems that are ongoing are being taken seriously by the institutions and officials and that the actions being taken could save lives. The use of technologies and the advancements of the information and research systems are making it easier to take the necessary steps to find and keep the bad people out of the building and, when necessary, review and remove those persons already inside the building. As someone who has been a part of the background investigation process for more than thirty years, I welcome these changes and updates that will provide you with the latest and best assistance and support in moving forward in school, college, and private-sector or government career opportunities. Take advantage of these new developments and opportunities by being truthful about your past, and take whatever steps are necessary to make changes in your life and move forward in confidence to fulfill your interest and dreams in life.

Another particularly important reason why businesses, companies, colleges, universities, state governments, and the federal government are using background investigations is the valuable information (history) disclosed about the person under consideration for employment or enrollment. As an example of what can happen when the background investigation process fails, consider the case of Edward Snowden. Snowden, a National Security Agency (NSA) contractor, allegedly stole more than 1.5 million top-secret NSA files and leaked classified information from the stolen files, which cost an unknown amount in damage to our global security. According to the NSA, Snowden's disclosures revealed numerous surveillance programs, some run by or through the NSA, Five Eyes Intelligence Alliance, telecommunication companies, and European governments. Five Eyes Intelligence Alliance consists of Australia, Canada, New Zealand, the United Kingdom, and the United States. Public records disclosed that these countries work in joint cooperation in signals intelligence through a long-standing agreement between the United Kingdom and the United States following World War II.

Snowden's background investigation was conducted through a government contractor, United Security Investigation Services (USIS).

Questions have been raised as to whether the investigation was conducted as mandated by the federal investigation process or if a portion of the report was filled with falsifications. There should have been red flags on his report due to, for example, Snowden not completing high school and his brief five-month service with the US Army Reserve. The red flags would have indicated issues in Snowden's background, allowing appropriate action to be taken to prevent security breaches. However, there were no red flags in Snowden's report, and he was given security access that he should have been denied. The case of Snowden has, of course, been the exception and not the normal outcome of a background investigation for a security clearance process with the federal government.

Another example of the necessary full background investigation is Bradley Manning (now Chelsea Manning), Private First Class, US Army, convicted of six offenses of violating the Espionage Act and one violation of the Computer Fraud and Abuse Act for disclosing portions of approximately 227 documents to WikiLeaks. Manning was charged as a spy and court-martialed for providing US government documents to persons not authorized to receive or view them in 2009 and 2010. This case has been viewed by many in the profession as an example of the essential need for additional investigative concerns with individuals assigned with multiple agencies of the government. It is also an example of how extensive the background investigations need to be, the important areas/sections to cover in the investigation, and the importance of the agreement between the contractor (third-party government contractor like USIS) and government departments (like the Office of Personnel Management) regarding the questions and responses, records review, reference interviews, and the candidate interview and follow-up notifications.

To further provide you with necessary information on this background investigation process, let us look at the following. The federal government conducts pre-employment background investigations for new government employees, as with many businesses. But the federal government process compared to the private corporations and businesses is more invasive. By that I mean that candidates must complete the Standard Form-86 (SF-86), a document that is usually between forty and one hundred pages. The depth and scope of the questionnaire is contingent on the candidate's level and type of security clearance. These levels of federal government security clearances are (1) Confidential, (2) Secret, and (3) Top Secret.

I would like to provide you with some factors to understanding the process you will be going through. There are four phases to the federal government's background investigation process: (1) questionnaire submission, (2) scheduling and initiation, (3) investigation, and (4) review. During this background investigation process, the assigned investigators will meet the candidate, their friends and neighbors, and others as requested. This adds to the element of verification, which makes the investigations more personal. Also, information regarding the candidate's personality, integrity, dependability, reliability, trustworthiness, and loyalty is documented for evaluation and adjudication.

To better assist you in understanding and being prepared through the background investigation process in completing your personnel security form (for consideration for employment with the US government), at the end of this chapter, I have provided you with important notes related to the online questionnaire and process—Standard Form 86 (SF-86)/e-QIP—(Electronic Questionnaires for Investigations Processing system). The e-QIP is a web-based automated system that was designed to facilitate the processing of standard investigative forms used when conducting background investigations for federal security, suitability, fitness, and credentialing purposes. e-QIP allows the user to electronically enter, update, and transmit their personal investigative data over a secure Internet connection to a requesting agency. It is used for new applicants for US government opportunities. When an individual has been given a conditional offer of employment, they must then complete the appropriate security questionnaire, usually a Standard Form 86 (SF-86)/e-QIP, Questionnaire for National Security Positions, and other required forms that provide full exception to the position of consideration. Conditional offers are not the norm today; only select positions within certain agencies and departments can extend this option for pre- or temporary employment. I have also provided a list of adjudicative guidelines as examples used by two of the US government agencies as they relate to security clearances for individuals seeking opportunities in the government.

As mentioned above, for those individuals who have been given a conditional offer of employment with the federal government, they must complete a Standard Form 86 (SF-86)/e-QIP. You must complete the questionnaire and other forms thoroughly and truthfully in response to questions of your past. The e-QIP can be overwhelming and intimidating at first, but each time you will have a better experience. After personally going through the security clearance process multiple times over the past thirty years, I have some helpful tips to make the process easier.

1. Review the sections and questions.
2. Collect and organize your personal files, documentation, and official data/papers.
3. Prepare your personal information to respond to each question in each section.
4. Prepare to be patient and take it step-by-step. This process will get easier as you navigate through each section with confidence.
5. Use the save button after the completion of your response to each question.
6. Remember that once you complete your e-QIP online and it is accepted, you will not have to see it again for five years. And the information requested the next time will start from the date you completed the e-QIP the last time and then move forward to the present.

Once you create your "profile" in the e-QIP systems, you will only have to update your information in the future.

Below are some suggestions and instructions for the e-QIP questionnaire to help you prepare in advance.

YOUR SECURITY CLEARANCE (GOVERNMENT, CORPORATE, AND CONTRACTORS)

According to the US government, a security clearance is an official determination that an individual is granted access to information that is classified by the government as (1) confidential, (2) secret, (3) top-secret.

The US government advises that security clearances are hierarchical; each level grants the holder of the security clearance access to information in that level (Secret) and the level below it (Confidential). Also be advised that having been granted this access to information, the location of this information (e.g., the Pentagon) can/may be a part of your final approval process.

In specific cases, a more in-depth background investigation will possibly involve examining tax and financial records, medical history, past travel and associates, and interviews with employers, colleagues, neighbors, friends, and family.

The intensity of the background investigation depends on the security clearance required for the job.

PERSONAL ASSISTANCE AND NAVIGATION THROUGH THE WINDOW OF TIME FOR YOUR BACKGROUND INVESTIGATION

You must provide a full ten years of residency history. Do not list residences prior to your eighteenth birthday unless necessary to provide a minimum of two years of residency history.

1. If you need to enter additional residences than the form provides, please use a continuation sheet/page.
2. Do *not* use P.O. Boxes. Entries in this section must be where you physically resided.

3. For each residence within the past three years, a person that knew you at that address is required.
4. Please select one of the following: neighbor, friend, landlord, business associate, or other.
5. Do *not* use "other" to list a relative as a verifier. Relatives (including in-laws) cannot be used as verifiers for this section.

ADDITIONAL REAL-TIME QUESTIONS AND RESPONSES FOR YOU

- List all schools you have attended, beginning with the most recent first and working back ten years. List college or university degrees and dates they were received. If your most recent degree or diploma, to include high school diploma, was received more than ten years ago, list it no matter when it was received.
- You must provide a full ten years of employment history or a history from your eighteenth birthday with no gaps. Do not list employments prior to your eighteenth birthday unless necessary to provide a minimum of two years of employment history. Any breaks in consecutive months of employment must be explained.
- If you need to enter additional employments than the form provides, please use a continuation sheet/page.
- If you make any unemployment entries, do *not* list yourself or the unemployment office as the verifier. The verifier can be a relative or spouse/cohabitant; it must be a person.
- If you make any self-employment entries, do *not* list yourself or a relative. List a partner or customer of your business.
- Males born after December 31, 1959, must enter their registration number or an authorized exemption reason. Go to http://www.sss.gov/ to look up your Selective Service number or the list of authorized exemptions (see the Who Must Register chart).
- The Selective Service number is *not* your Social Security number. Even if you think you have an exemption, look it up anyway. Do *not* assume you have an exemption.

- Your Military Service number is your SSN unless you were in the service prior to 1972.
- You must provide *all* information for your three personal references. The references must be people you presently know. If you cannot obtain this information, they are not suitable references for this section.
- Individuals that you use in this section cannot be used as verifiers in any other section. These individuals' combined association with you must cover the past seven years, including up to present day.
- You must provide a Social Security number if your current spouse/cohabitant's country of citizenship is the United States.
- You must provide an entry for "Other Names Used" by spouse if your current spouse's last name is not their maiden name.
- You must provide an entry for your in-laws if you are married. Provide as much information as possible. For unknown information, you must provide a detailed explanation as to why you are unable to provide the information.
- Do *not* omit entries for relatives because they are deceased, not close to you, or you lack some information. You will be able to indicate deceased or explain why you are missing certain information on a separate sheet if needed.
- If you make an entry for a living relative born in a foreign country, who is also a US citizen, you must enter at least one of the listed document numbers or strongly explain in your comments why you are unable to obtain the number after making a good-faith effort.
- Do *not* use the "many short trips" note to avoid making multiple entries for separate visits to the same country over the course of many years or for different countries visited. This note is intended for border crossings near where you permanently reside.
- Do not list debts that you are current on. Only provide if you answer yes to questions in Section 26.1–26.7.
- You must provide complete information for all entries for a debt. Do *not* enter a response such as "I don't know."

- Do *not* enter incomplete addresses. Look up the address of the court or bank on their website.
- Look up information on your credit report (https://www.annualcredit report.com/cra/index.jsp).

After taking the time to read this chapter, I would like for you to ask yourself, "What are my concerns regarding the background investigation process as it pertains to my past and what is my current situation and future moving forward?"

QUESTIONS TO CONSIDER

1. What are the things I need to do in order to be ready for my background investigation?
2. What do I need to know concerning investigative reports about me?
3. Why is the background investigation important for me?
4. Given the information in this chapter, how should I prepare for my investigative inquiry/questionnaire and my background check/ investigation?
5. Do any of the concerns and/or issues listed in this chapter apply to me?
6. How well do I understand the information provided to me in this chapter?

7

How to Prepare for Your Background Investigation

When you know you are going to be applying for college or a job in the corporate or government sectors, take the following steps to reduce the chances that you and/or the potential college/employer will be surprised or caught off guard by information found in your background investigations.

Global communications that connect us together, both "positive and negative."
Prasit Photo/Moment via Getty Images

RECOMMENDATIONS

Conduct Your Own Background Investigation
In order for you to see and know what a college's or employer's background investigation might uncover, check out the services of several

online companies and/or other investigators that specialize in background investigations and request they conduct one for you. By doing this, you can discover if the data bases of information contain erroneous or misleading information. Or you can use one of the many online search services to find out what an employer would learn if conducting a background investigation in this way.

For young adults, I will say that one of the most important actions you can take prior to a background investigation is to conduct a complete review of your social media profile, including but not limited to Facebook, Instagram, Twitter, Snapchat, and LinkedIn. Most government agencies and companies now review candidates' profiles with or without their knowledge. They look for inappropriate and unprofessional pictures, profane statuses, your comments on shared content, and how your profile matches the candidate presented on your resume and application. After reviewing your social media profile, edit or delete images and content that would not be viewed as positive or favorable for you.

Read the Fine Print Carefully!

Once you sign a college acceptance letter or employment application, you will be asked to sign a consent form if a background investigation is required. It is *your* responsibility to read this statement carefully and ask questions if the authorization statement is not clear. Unfortunately, most applicants are in an awkward position since refusing to authorize a background check may jeopardize the chances of getting the job. Notice of a background investigation has to be on a separate form. The only other information this form can include is your authorization and information that identifies who you are. Neither the notice of a background investigation nor any other form should ask questions about race, sex, full date of birth, or maiden name. Such questions violate the federal Equal Employment Opportunity laws. And you should not be asked to sign any document that waives your right to sue a screening company (third party) or the employer for violations of the law.

Conduct a Review of All Your Digital Information
Available through the World Wide Web

You should conduct a search on your name—in quotation marks—in the major search engines such as Google and Yahoo. If you find unflattering references, contact the website to learn if and how you can remove them. You can monitor the web for new mentions of your name by setting up a Google Alert (http://www.google.com/alerts). Google Alert will send you e-mail updates of the latest Google results mentioning your name. The following search engines are recommended to find out more about yourself (they include social media and e-mail addresses as well as relatives and associates): www.beenverified.com and www.truthfinder.com. These are two of best of all the online sites on the web. I have used both with successful results and recommend them.

KNOWLEDGE POINT

You should not underestimate the power of your online reputation to sway potential employers. Many employers are turning to third-party screening companies such as Social Intelligence to monitor and report on a potential employee's social networking activity. Understand that if employers themselves monitor your Internet activity, you do not have rights under the Fair Credit Reporting Act.

Order a Copy of Your Credit Report

It is your responsibility to know that something you do not recognize or that you disagree with has been resolved prior to a potential employer inquiry. Your knowledge of the information disclosed will allow you to dispute the information with the creditor and/or credit bureau before you have to explain it to the interviewer. A common discovery is that another individual's name may appear on your credit report. This happens when someone mistakenly writes down the wrong Social Security number on a credit application, causing that name to appear on your file. Or you might be a victim of identity theft and not even know about it.

I recommend you get an annual report through www.annualcredit report.com. This report combines the credit information of Experian, Equifax, and Transunion into one report with all the contact information and response options.

Conduct a Review of Any Court Documents and/or Records Regarding Your Past Charges and Sentences

For actions that resulted in an arrest or any legal matter that involved court case(s), you will need to go to the court (city, county, state, or federal) where this took place and review the files. Make sure the listed information is correct and up-to-date. Some reporting agencies often report felony convictions when the person honestly believes the crime was reduced to a misdemeanor or a misdemeanor conviction when the person thought the charge was reduced to an infraction. Court records are not always updated correctly. For example, a signature by a judge that was needed to reduce the charges might not have been obtained or recorded by the court. You should not rely on what someone else may have told you. If you think the conviction was expunged or dismissed, get a certified copy of your report from the court where the offense occurred. A recommended site is www.checkmate.com, which includes criminal records and court-related records.

Conduct a Review of All Department of Motor Vehicles Records in All the States You Have Lived and Obtained a License

You must request a copy of your driving record from the Department of Motor Vehicles, especially if you are applying for a job that involves driving. Most employers ask on their application if you were ever convicted of a crime. Some will word the question to ask whether you have ever been convicted of a felony or misdemeanor.

Typically, the application says you do not have to divulge a case that was expunged or dismissed or that was a minor traffic violation. Understand that a "driving under the influence" (DUI) or "driving while intoxicated" (DWI) conviction is not considered a minor traffic infraction in the United States. All applicants with a DUI or DWI who have not checked "yes" on a job application may be denied employment for falsifying the form or providing false and misleading information, even when the incident occurred only once or happened many years before. The potential employer may perceive this as dishonesty, even though the applicant might only have been confused by the question. Check your state's website for specific information regarding this process.

I cannot stress enough how important it is to review your application to make sure it is completely true and accurate. Make sure that everything is correct to the best of your knowledge and then make sure the information is understandable—do not try to use words that are unclear and confusing. False and misleading information will delay the process and will lead to concerns and issues regarding your truthfulness and integrity as a candidate seeking employment with a company and/or the government. Some of the examples I have seen from time to time are education degrees, work employers and dates of employment, gaps of thirty days or more with no information provided, and references listed that do not really know you and cannot comment on your character for a position of trust and responsibility with the government. Think of your background investigation as that big event, that first time in the spotlight, because it is your opportunity to get something you want—an education, a job, a career, your time to be in charge of your life. As I have stated in previous chapters, the key is your preparation. Do what it takes to complete a thorough review of your past and your current life activities and events.

A reminder to each of you: when you know that there is something that might show up or be shared by another person during your background investigation, it would be advantageous for you to discuss this concern or issue with your sponsoring company or agency prior to the start of the investigation. Issues and problems that have been fully discussed and resolved or addressed in a substantive manner are usually the clearest event or item to disclosed. An example of this type of issue or problem could be that you were a passenger in a vehicle that was stopped for speeding in a city where you used to live during your senior year in high school (you were eighteen years old) and you were charged with underage drinking. Only your friends from that place and time know about this incident, and the records may or may not be available or maintained regarding that event. Sometimes recorded information taken by the police or sheriff's deputies regarding this type of incident for someone who has just turned eighteen years old may not be in the criminal data base (this will vary from jurisdictions to jurisdictions around the country).

YOUR HISTORY IS YOUR BACKGROUND

The background investigation process starts on paper and a computer keyboard at this time in your life; however, there are some exceptions depending on certain types of events (arrests, convictions) that have taken place from early childhood. Some of these events may include theft, robbery, and other charges that would be listed on the status of a minor. The purpose of writing this book is to help inform students in high school and their early years of college about some of the basic actions, events, and situations that will determine your entry in college, the military, and any job opportunities whether in the corporate sector or in government services. Your personal actions and decisions starting in elementary school, junior high school, and throughout your high school years will determine whether you will be accepted in college and what opportunities you are eligible for even with a college degree. In the background investigation process, your personal decisions about who you select as friends; places you decide to visit after hours; your interactions with friends, neighbors, and family; and your personal interests and habits you develop in life will be revealed.

From your eighteenth birthday forward, your past becomes a major part of your future opportunities in the real world of government and corporate communities. Your understanding of life principles and the teachings and guidance of your parents, counselors, and advisors will determine your decision-making process through various steps from childhood through adulthood.

Just do this in all your interactions with others and through the processes in life.
jayk7/Moment via Getty Images

A NOTE FOR THOSE WITH SERIOUS CONCERNS ABOUT THEIR PAST

As human beings, we are not perfect and will by nature make mistakes (some minor, others major) as we grow up from children to adults. Your past is your history; you cannot change your past and therefore must be able and willing to live in the present and learn from your mistakes and negative events of your past. How you choose to present yourself today or tomorrow will have parts of your history in that presentation and character.

Remember, you create and develop your history through all the actions and events every day of your life. The people involved in making decisions regarding background investigation and security clearance applications were once your age and experienced many of the same events you have experienced or will experience as you become adults. Those individuals use the policy and procedures in making each final decision on the applicant based on the person's truthfulness when responding to all questions about their past history. I must emphasize to you that you can be your best representative of the truth when discussing your past actions.

QUESTIONS TO CONSIDER

1. Based on the information provided, are you ready to conduct your own background review?
2. What are some of the important concerns, events, and issues you will find?
3. Are you still dealing with some of these activities in your current life?
4. What are the next steps you have to take to make necessary changes in your life?
5. How does the information and facts provided help you to prepare for the investigative review, background check, and/or background investigation?
6. What will you do with the knowledge that you have learned from this chapter to help you in your life activities and objectives?
7. What is your new view and assessment of yourself in order to be the person you want to be?
8. What are the changes and corrections you have made in your life to move forward?

8

How the US Government Conducts Your Background Investigation

The information provided in this chapter has been pulled from investigative notes, documents, forms, and examples used by the US Departments of Defense, Homeland Security, and Justice and the Office of Personnel Management. The following guidelines are established for all US government civilian and military personnel, consultants, contractors, employees of contractors, licensees, certificate holders or grantees and their employees, and other individuals who require access to classified information. The requirements apply to all persons being considered for initial or continued eligibility for access to classified information, to include sensitive compartmented information and special access programs, and are to be used by government departments and agencies in *all* final clearance determinations.

THE WAY THE ADJUDICATIVE PROCESS WORKS

The adjudicative process is an examination of a period of a person's life to determine that the person is an acceptable security risk. Eligibility for access to classified information is based on the individual meeting these personnel security guidelines. The adjudication process is the careful weighing of several variables known as the "whole person" concept. All available, reliable information about the person, past and present, favorable and unfavorable, should be considered in reaching a determination. In evaluating the relevance of a candidate's conduct, the adjudicator should consider the following factors:

1. What is the nature, extent, and seriousness of the conduct in question?
2. What are the circumstances surrounding the conduct in question, to include your knowledgeable participation?
3. What is the frequency and recency of the conduct in question?
4. What is the individual's age and maturity (teenager/adult) at the time of the conduct?
5. What is the voluntariness of participation?
6. What is the presence or absence of rehabilitation and other permanent behavioral changes of the conduct in question?
7. What is the motivation for the conduct in question?
8. What is the potential for pressure, coercion, exploitation, or duress of the conduct in question?
9. What is the likelihood of continuation or recurrence of the conduct in question?
10. What is the final evaluation to these responses by the candidate in question?

Each case must be judged on its own merits, and final determination remains the responsibility of the specific department or agency. Any doubt concerning personnel being considered for access to classified information will be resolved in favor of the national security and considered final.

The ultimate determination of the granting or continuing of eligibility for a security clearance must be clearly consistent with the interests of national security and an overall commonsense determination based upon careful consideration of the following:

1. allegiance to the United States;
2. foreign influence;

3. foreign preference;
4. personal conduct;
5. financial considerations;
6. alcohol consumption;
7. drug involvement;
8. sexual behavior;
9. emotional, mental, and personality disorders;
10. criminal conduct;
11. security violations;
12. outside activities; and
13. misuse of information technology systems.

The process reviews each of the above points and should be evaluated in the context of the whole person. Although negative information concerning a single point may not be enough for an unfavorable determination, the candidate may be disqualified if available information reflects a recent or recurring pattern of questionable judgment, irresponsibility, or emotionally unstable behavior.

Understand that when information of security concern becomes known about a candidate who is currently eligible for access to classified information, the adjudicator will consider whether the person:

1. voluntarily reported the information;
2. sought assistance and followed professional guidance, where appropriate;
3. resolved or appears likely to favorably resolve the security concern;
4. has demonstrated positive changes in behavior and employment; or
5. should have his or her access temporarily suspended pending final adjudication of the information.

When, after evaluating information of security concern, the adjudicator decides that the information is not serious enough to warrant a recommendation of disapproval or revocation of the security clearance, it may be appropriate to recommend approval with a warning that future incidents of a similar nature may resort in withdrawing access.

1. YOUR ALLEGIANCE TO THE UNITED STATES

A candidate must be of unquestioned allegiance to the United States. The willingness to safeguard classified information is in doubt if there is any reason to suspect an individual's allegiance to the United States.

The circumstances and conditions that could raise a security concern and may be disqualifying include:

1. Are you involved in any act of sabotage, espionage, treason, terrorism, sedition, or other act whose aim is to overthrow the government of the United States or alter the form of government by unconstitutional means?
2. Are you involved in any association or sympathy with persons who are attempting to commit, or who are committing, any of the above acts?
3. Do you have any association or sympathy with persons or organizations that advocate the overthrow of the US government, or any state or subdivision, by force or violence or by other unconstitutional means?
4. Do you have any involvement in activities that unlawfully advocate or practice the commission of acts of force or violence to prevent others from exercising their rights under the Constitution or laws of the United States or of any state?

The circumstances and conditions that could reduce security concerns include:

1. Was the candidate unaware of the unlawful aims of the person or organization and severed ties upon learning of these?
2. Was the candidate's involvement only with the lawful or humanitarian aspects of such an organization?

3. Was the candidate's involvement in the above activities for only a short period of time and attributable to curiosity or academic interest?
4. Has the candidate had any recent involvement or association with such activities?

2. YOUR FOREIGN INFLUENCE

A security risk may exist when a candidate's immediate family, including cohabitant, and other persons to whom he or she may be bound by affection, influence, or obligation: (1) are not citizens of the United States or (2) may be subject to duress. These situations could create the potential for foreign influence that could result in the compromise of classified information. Contacts with citizens of other countries or financial interests in other countries are also relevant to security determinations if they make a candidate potentially vulnerable to coercion, exploitation, or pressure.

The circumstances and conditions that could raise a security concern and may be disqualifying include:

1. your immediate family member, or a person to whom you have close ties of affection or obligation, is a citizen of, or resident or present in, a foreign country;
2. the sharing of living quarters with a person or persons, regardless of their citizenship status, if the potential for adverse foreign influence or duress exists;
3. your relatives, cohabitant, or associates who relate to any foreign government;
4. you are failing to report, where required, associations with foreign nationals;
5. any unauthorized association with a suspected or known collaborator or employee of a foreign intelligence service;
6. any conduct that may make you vulnerable to coercion, exploitation, or pressure by a foreign government;

7. any indications that representatives or nationals from a foreign country are acting to increase the vulnerability of the candidate to possible future exploitation, coercion, or pressure; or

8. having a substantial financial interest in a country or in any foreign-owned or -operated business that could make the candidate vulnerable to foreign influence.

The circumstances and conditions that could reduce security concerns include the following:

1. The determination that the immediate family member(s), cohabitant, or associate(s) in question would not constitute an unacceptable security risk.

2. Any contacts with foreign citizens are the result of official US government business.

3. Any contact and correspondence with foreign citizens are casual and infrequent.

4. The individual has promptly reported to proper authorities all contacts, requests, or threats from persons or organizations from a foreign country, as required.

5. Any foreign financial interests are minimal and not enough to affect the individual's security responsibilities.

3. YOUR FOREIGN PREFERENCE

When a candidate acts in such a way as to indicate a preference for a foreign country over the United States, then he or she may be prone to provide information or make decisions that are harmful to the interests of the United States.

The circumstances and conditions that could raise a security concern and may be disqualifying include:

1. an exercise of dual citizenship;

2. the possession and/or use of a foreign passport;

3. any military service or a willingness to bear arms for a foreign country;
4. the acceptance of educational, medical, or other benefits, such as retirement and social welfare, from a foreign country;
5. a residence in a foreign country to meet citizenship requirements;
6. the use of foreign citizenship to protect financial or business interests in another country;
7. the seeking or holding of political office in a foreign country;
8. your voting in foreign elections; or
9. the performing or attempting to perform duties, or otherwise acting, so as to serve the interests of another government in preference to the interests of the United States.

The circumstances and conditions that could reduce security concerns include:

1. The use of dual citizenship is based solely on parents' citizenship or birth in a foreign country.
2. Any indicators of possible foreign preference (e.g., foreign military service) occurred before obtaining US citizenship.
3. Any activity is sanctioned by the United States.
4. The candidate has expressed a willingness to renounce dual citizenship.

4. YOUR PERSONAL CONDUCT

Conduct involving questionable judgment, untrustworthiness, unreliability, or unwillingness to comply with rules and regulations could indicate that the person may not properly safeguard classified information.

The following will normally result in an unfavorable clearance action or administrative termination of further processing for clearance eligibility:

1. your refusal to undergo or cooperate with required security processing, including medical and psychological testing; or
2. your refusal to complete required security forms and releases or provide full, frank, and truthful answers to lawful questions of investigators, security officials, or other official representatives in connection with a personnel security or trustworthiness determination.

The circumstances and conditions that could raise a security concern and may be disqualifying also include:

1. the reliable, unfavorable information provided by associates, employers, coworkers, neighbors, and other acquaintances;
2. the deliberate omission, concealment, or falsification of relevant and material facts from any personnel security questionnaire, personal history statement, or similar form used to conduct investigations, determine employment qualifications, award benefits or status, determine security clearance eligibility or trustworthiness, or award fiduciary responsibilities;
3. deliberately providing false or misleading information concerning relevant and material matters to an investigator, security official, competent medical authority, or other official representative in connection with a personnel security or trustworthiness determination;
4. personal conduct or concealment of information that increases a candidate's vulnerability to coercion, exploitation, or pressure;
5. a (your) pattern of dishonesty or rule violations; or
6. the (your) association with persons involved in criminal activity.

The circumstances and conditions that could reduce security concerns include:

1. The information was unsubstantiated or not pertinent to a determination of judgment, trustworthiness, or reliability.

2. The falsification was an isolated incident and was not recent, and the candidate has subsequently provided correct information voluntarily.
3. The candidate made prompt, good-faith efforts to correct the falsification before being confronted with the facts.
4. The omission of material facts was caused or significantly contributed to by improper or inadequate advice of authorized personnel, and the previously omitted information was promptly and fully provided.
5. The candidate has taken positive steps to significantly reduce or eliminate vulnerability to coercion, exploitation, or pressure.
6. The refusal to cooperate was based on advice from legal counsel or other officials that the candidate was not required to comply with security processing requirements and, upon being made aware of the requirement, the candidate fully and truthfully provided the requested information.
7. Any association with persons involved in criminal activities has ceased.

5. YOUR FINANCIAL CONSIDERATIONS

A candidate who is financially overextended is at risk of having to engage in illegal acts to generate funds. Unexplained affluence is often linked to proceeds from financially profitable criminal acts.

The circumstances and conditions that could raise a security concern and may be disqualifying include:

1. your history of not meeting financial obligations;
2. deceptive or illegal financial practices such as embezzlement, employee theft, check fraud, income tax evasion, expense account fraud, filing deceptive loan statements, and other intentional financial breaches of trust;
3. your inability or unwillingness to satisfy debts;
4. your unexplained affluence; or

5. your financial problems that are linked to gambling, drug abuse, alcoholism, or other issues of security concern.

The circumstances and conditions that could reduce security concerns include:

1. Your behavior was not recent.
2. This was an isolated incident.
3. The conditions that resulted in the behavior were largely beyond the person's control (e.g., loss of employment, a business downturn, unexpected medical emergency, or a death, divorce, or separation).
4. The candidate has received or is receiving counseling for the problem, and there are clear indications that the problem is being resolved or is under control.
5. The affluence resulted from a legal source.
6. The individual initiated a good-faith effort to repay overdue creditors or otherwise resolve debts.

6. YOUR ALCOHOL CONSUMPTION

Excessive alcohol consumption often leads to the exercise of questionable judgment, unreliability, and failure to control impulses and increases the risk of unauthorized disclosure of classified information due to carelessness.

The circumstances and conditions that could raise a security concern and may be disqualifying include:

1. any alcohol-related incidents away from work, such as driving while under the influence, fighting, child or spouse abuse, or other criminal incidents related to alcohol use;
2. any alcohol-related incidents at work, such as reporting for work or duty in an intoxicated or impaired condition or drinking on the job;
3. any diagnosis by a credentialed medical professional of alcohol abuse or alcohol dependence;

4. any habitual or binge consumption of alcohol to the point of impaired judgment; or

5. any consumption of alcohol subsequent to a diagnosis of alcoholism by a credentialed medical professional and following completion of an alcohol rehabilitation program.

The circumstances and conditions that could reduce security concerns include:

1. The alcohol-related incidents do not indicate a pattern.

2. The problem occurred a few years ago, and there is no indication of a recent problem.

3. Positive changes in behavior are supportive of sobriety.

4. The candidate has successfully completed inpatient or outpatient rehabilitation along with aftercare requirements, participates frequently in meetings of Alcoholics Anonymous or a similar organization, abstained from alcohol for a period of at least twelve months, and received a favorable prognosis by a credentialed medical professional.

7. YOUR DRUG USE AND PERSONAL INVOLVEMENT

Any improper or illegal involvement with drugs raises questions regarding a candidate's willingness or ability to protect classified information. Drug abuse or dependence may impair social or occupational functioning, increasing the risk of an unauthorized disclosure of classified information. Drugs are defined as mood and behavior altering and include:

1. any drugs, materials, and other chemical compounds identified and listed in the Controlled Substances Act of 1970, as amended (e.g., marijuana or cannabis, depressants, narcotics, stimulants, and hallucinogens), and

2. any inhalants and other similar substances. Drug abuse is the illegal use of a drug or use of a legal drug in a manner that deviates from approved medical direction.

The circumstances and conditions that could raise a security concern and may be disqualifying include:

1. any drug abuse (see above definition);
2. any illegal drug possession, including cultivation, processing, manufacture, purchase, sale, or distribution; or
3. the failure to successfully complete a drug treatment program prescribed by a credentialed medical professional.

Current drug involvement, especially following the granting of a security clearance, or an expressed intent not to discontinue use will normally result in an unfavorable determination.

The circumstances and conditions that could reduce security concerns include:

1. Your drug involvement was not recent.
2. Your drug involvement was an isolated or infrequent event.
3. You demonstrated intent not to abuse any drugs in the future.
4. Your satisfactory completion of a drug treatment program prescribed by a credentialed medical professional.

8. YOUR SEXUAL BEHAVIOR

Sexual behavior is a security concern if it involves a criminal offense, indicates a personality or emotional disorder, subjects the individual to undue influence or coercion, or reflects lack of judgment or discretion. (Sexual orientation or preference may not be used as a basis for or as a disqualifying factor in determining a person's eligibility for a security clearance.)

The circumstances and conditions that could raise a security concern and may be disqualifying include:

1. sexual behavior of a criminal nature, whether the candidate has been prosecuted;
2. compulsive or addictive sexual behavior when the person is unable to stop a pattern of self-destructive or high-risk behavior or that is symptomatic of a personality disorder;
3. sexual behavior that causes a candidate to be vulnerable to undue influence or coercion; or
4. sexual behavior of a public nature and/or that reflects lack of discretion or judgment.

The circumstances and conditions that could reduce security concerns include:

1. The behavior occurred during or prior to adolescence, and there is no evidence of subsequent conduct of a similar nature.
2. The behavior was not recent, and there is no evidence of subsequent conduct of a similar nature.
3. There is no other evidence of questionable judgment, irresponsibility, or emotional instability.
4. The behavior no longer serves as a basis for undue influence or coercion.

9. YOUR EMOTIONAL, MENTAL, AND PERSONALITY DISORDERS

Emotional, mental, and personality disorders can cause a significant deficit in a candidate's psychological, social, and occupational functioning. These disorders are of security concern because they may indicate a fault in judgment, reliability, or stability.

When appropriate, a credentialed mental health professional, acceptable to or approved by the government, should be consulted so that potentially disqualifying and mitigating information may be fully and rigorously evaluated.

The circumstances and conditions that could raise a security concern and may be disqualifying include:

1. diagnosis by a credentialed mental health professional that the candidate has a disorder that could result in a defect in psychological, social, or occupational functioning;
2. information that suggests that a candidate has failed to follow appropriate medical advice relating to treatment of a diagnosed disorder (e.g., failure to take prescribed medication);
3. a pattern of high-risk, irresponsible, aggressive, antisocial, or emotionally unstable behavior; or
4. information that suggests that the candidate's current behavior indicates a defect in his or her judgment or reliability.

The circumstances and conditions that could reduce security concerns include:

1. There is no indication of a current problem.
2. A credentialed mental health professional recently diagnosed that a candidate's previous emotional, mental, or personality disorder is cured or in remission and has a low probability of recurrence or exacerbation.
3. The past emotional instability was a temporary condition (e.g., one caused by a death, illness, or marital breakup), the situation has been resolved, and the individual is no longer emotionally unstable.

10. YOUR CRIMINAL CONDUCT

A history or pattern of criminal activity creates doubt about a person's judgment, reliability, and trustworthiness.

The circumstances and conditions that could raise a security concern and may be disqualifying include:

1. any criminal conduct, regardless of whether the person was formally charged, or
2. a single serious crime or multiple lesser offenses.

The circumstances and conditions that could reduce security concerns include:

1. The criminal behavior was not recent.
2. The crime was an isolated incident.
3. The person was pressured or coerced into committing the act, and those pressures are no longer present in that person's life.
4. The person did not voluntarily commit the act, and/or the factors leading to the violation are not likely to recur.
5. There is clear evidence of successful rehabilitation.

11. YOUR SECURITY VIOLATIONS

Noncompliance with security regulations raises doubt about an individual's trustworthiness, willingness, and ability to safeguard classified information.

The circumstances and conditions that could raise a security concern and may be disqualifying include:

1. unauthorized disclosure of classified information, or
2. any violations that are deliberate or multiple or due to negligence.

The circumstances and conditions that could reduce security concerns include:

1. The actions were inadvertent.
2. The actions were isolated or infrequent.
3. The actions were due to improper or inadequate training.
4. The actions demonstrate a positive attitude toward the discharge of security responsibilities.

12. YOUR OUTSIDE ACTIVITIES—PEOPLE AND PLACES

The involvement in certain types of outside employment or activities is of security concern if it poses a conflict with an individual's security responsibilities and could create an increased risk of unauthorized disclosure of classified information.

The circumstances and conditions that could raise a security concern and may be disqualifying include any service, whether compensated, volunteer, or employment, with:

1. travel to a foreign country;
2. contact with any foreign nationals;
3. contact with a representative of any foreign interest; or
4. contact/involvement with any foreign, domestic, or international organization or person engaged in analysis, discussion, or publication of material on intelligence, defense, foreign affairs, or protected technology.

The circumstances and conditions that could reduce security concerns include:

1. The complete evaluation of the outside employment or activity indicates that it does not pose a conflict with a candidate's security responsibilities.
2. The candidate terminates the employment or discontinues the activity upon being notified that it is in conflict with his or her security responsibilities.

13. YOUR MISUSE OF INFORMATION TECHNOLOGY SYSTEMS

Noncompliance with rules, procedures, guidelines, or regulations pertaining to information technology systems may raise security concerns about an individual's trustworthiness, willingness, and ability to properly protect classified systems, networks, and information.

Information technology systems include all related equipment used for the communication, transmission, processing, manipulation, and storage of classified or sensitive information.

The circumstances and conditions that could raise a security concern and may be disqualifying include:

1. the illegal or unauthorized entry into any information technology system;
2. the illegal or unauthorized modification, destruction, manipulation, or denial of access to information residing on an information technology system;
3. the removal (or use) of hardware, software, or media from any information technology system without authorization or when specifically prohibited by rules, procedures, guidelines, or regulations; or
4. the introduction of hardware, software, or media into any information technology system without authorization or when specifically prohibited by rules, procedures, guidelines, or regulations.

The circumstances and conditions that could reduce security concerns include:

1. The misuse was not recent or significant.
2. The conduct was unintentional or inadvertent.
3. The introduction or removal of media was authorized.
4. The misuse was an isolated event.
5. The misuse was followed by a prompt, good-faith effort to correct the situation.

Bibliography

Annual Credit Report. "Credit Reports." Last modified December 2020. http://www.annualcreditreport.com.

Barnhart, Brent. "The Most Important Instagram Statistics You Need to Know for 2021." Sprout Social. Last modified February 25, 2021. https://sproutsocial.com/insights/Instagram-stats/.

Beenverified. "People Search." Last modified 2020. http: //www.beenverified .com.

Bonnie. R. J., and M. E. O'Connell, editors. *Reducing Underage Drinking: A Collective Responsibility.* Washington, D.C.: National Academies Press, 2004. https://pubmed.ncbi.nlm.nih.gov/20669473/.

Center for Behavioral Health Statistics and Quality. *Results from the 2016 National Survey on Drug Use and Health: Detailed Tables.* Rockville, MD: External Substance Abuse and Mental Health Services Administration, 2017. https://www.samhsa.gov/data/sites/default/files/NSDUH-DetTabs -2016/NSDUH-DetTabs-2016.pdf.

Centers for Disease Control and Prevention (CDC). "Alcohol-Related Disease Impact (ARDI)." Last modified September 3, 2020. https://nccd.cdc.gov /DPH_ARDI/default/default.aspx.

Checkmate. "Background Checks." Last modified December 2020. http://www.checkmate.com.

Federal Bureau of Investigations. "Background Investigations." Last modified January 2021. http://www.fbi.gov.

Google. "Google Alerts." Last modified June 25, 2020. http://www.google.com/alerts.

Greenwald, Glenn. "Edward Snowden: The Whistleblower behind the NSA Surveillance Revelations." *The Guardian*, June 9, 2013.

Iqbal, Mansoor. "Snapchat Revenue and Usage Statistics (2020)." Business of Apps. Last modified February 12, 2021. https://www.businessofapps.com/data/snapchat-statistics/.

Johnston, L. D., R. A. Miech, P. M. O'Malley, J. E. Schulenberg, and M. E. Patrick . *Monitoring the Future National Survey Results on Drug Use, 1975–2017: 2017 Overview: Key Findings on Adolescent Drug Use*. Ann Arbor: Institute for Social Research, University of Michigan, 2018. http://monitoringthefuture.org/pubs/monographs/mtf-overview2017.pdf.

Kann, L., T. McManus, and W. A. Harris et al. "Youth Risk Behavior Surveillance—United States, 2017." *Morbidity and Mortality Weekly Report Surveillance Summaries* 67, no. 8 (June 15, 2018): 1–114. https://www.cdc.gov/mmwr/volumes/67/ss/ss6708a1.htm?s_cid=ss6708a1_w.

Keteyian, Armen. "Out of Bounds: College Athletes and Crime." CBS and *Sports Illustrated*, March 3, 2011.

Market.us. "Facebook Statistics and Facts." Last modified January 28, 2021. http://www.market.us/statistics/social-media/facebook/.

Miller, J. W., T. S. Naimi, R. D. Brewer, and S. E. Jones. "Binge Drinking and Associated Health Risk Behaviors among High School Students." *Pediatrics* 119, no. 1 (2007): 76–85. https://pubmed.ncbi.nlm.nih.gov/17200273/.

Naeger, S. "Emergency Department Visits involving Underage Alcohol Use: 2010 to 2013." *The CBHSQ Report*, May 16, 2017. https://www.samhsa.gov/data/sites/default/files/report_3061/ShortReport-3061.html.

National Security Agency (NSA). "Signals Intelligence (SIGINT) and Computer Network Operations (CNO)." Last modified 2020. https://www.nsa.gov/.

Office of Juvenile Justice and Delinquency Prevention. *Drinking in America: Myths, Realities, and Prevention Policy*. Washington, D.C.: U.S. Department of Justice, Office of Justice Programs, Office of Juvenile Justice and Delinquency Prevention, 2005. http://citeseerx.ist.psu.edu/viewdoc /summary?doi=10.1.1.370.5335.

Office of Personnel Management (OPM). "Background Investigation/ Standard 86 and e-QIP." Last modified October 1, 2019. http://www .opm.gov.

Omnicore. "Twitter by the Numbers: Stats, Demographics, and Fun Facts." Last modified January 6, 2021. https://www.omnicoreagency.com/twitter -statistics/.

Sacks, J. J., K. R. Gonzales, E. E. Bouchery, L. E. Tomedi, and R. D. Brewer. "2010 National and State Costs of Excessive Alcohol Consumption." *American Journal of Preventive Medicine* 49, no. 5 (2015): e73–e79. https:// pubmed.ncbi.nlm.nih.gov/26477807/.

Substance Abuse and Mental Health Services Administration. *Report to Congress on the Prevention and Reduction of Underage Drinking*. Rockville, MD: US Department of Health and Human Services, 2017. https://www .stopalcoholabuse.gov/media/ReportToCongress/2017/report_main/stop _act_rtc_2017.pdf.

Truthfinder. "Public Record." Last modified 2020. http://www.truthfinder.com.

US Department of Health and Human Services. *The Surgeon General's Call to Action to Prevent and Reduce Underage Drinking*. Rockville, MD: US Department of Health and Human Services, 2007. https://www.ncbi.nlm .nih.gov/books/NBK44360/.

US Department of State. "Background Investigations." Last modified September 23, 2020. http://www.state.gov.

About the Author

Anthony Oatis has served as a special agent and special investigator for the US Department of Defense, US Department of State, US Department of Homeland Security, and US Department of Justice. He has also worked as a security consultant to several businesses and companies over the past thirty-three years. His background is in criminal justice, political science, and background investigation and security. Anthony has a master's degree in political science and is the founder of Think Right Global Solutions. Through his law enforcement and security networks, he currently works in the Atlanta, Georgia; Orlando, Florida; St. Louis, Missouri; and Washington, D.C., metro areas providing information, resources, and presentations about the background investigation process and current security requirements and activities to both high school and college students.